I0840972

TRUTH ABOUT PEOPLE

They're Social, You're Independent

Karen Kellock Ph.D.

Manual for Superior Men

This is a complete theory based on Einstein physics, Political Psychology, Systems Theory and Archetypal Psychiatry.

FORMULA

All success attraction
All disease obstruction
All recovery elimination

You must fast on all three

OBSTRUCTIONS:

People
Habit
Food

THE TRUTH ABOUT PEOPLE

The ruthless gossiping/petty competitions in a small liberal town: I'm a survivor, wow.   They incited riots, they came to my house, always with an army of monkeys of course.   Once pegged it's impossible to change the image for years it seems.   Sick family system extends out. The sisters lay evil seeds and the system repeats itself.   Little lady seems harmless, right? She is NOT. She has the power of the sheriff who she calls a lot.

TRUTH ABOUT PEOPLE

COMMON SYMPTOMS MAKE CLEAR
THEY WEAR US DOWN
PETTY COMPETITIONS
SOCIAL WAS LIKE A PRISON
ESCAPING TO A GHOST TOWN
MOM SAID "GIVE HIM THE BELT"
ENTER WORLD SUCCESS
THE TRUTH ABOUT PEOPLE
ELDER CONSCIOUSNESS
SMALL TOWN HIX/SOCIAL TRICKS
TRAUMATIZED BY CRIME
TIME GOES ON, GENERATIONS PASS
HUMILIATION PRECEDES TRANSFORMATION
WIFE OF ALCOHOLIC SYNDROME
THEY STEAL PIECES OF YOU
MODERN SOCIETY IS LOGORRHAIC
FEMALECENTRIC FALSE CHURCHES
MEN CAVE INTO LIBERAL WIVES
ALL DEPARTMENTS FEMALECENTRIC
CALUMNY AND SOUL MURDER
PSYCHOPATHS ARE ABOUT BASIC FUNCTIONS
REPENTANCE RAISES ARCHETYPE *WAY* UP
SUFFERING & OVEREXCITABILITY = GROWTH
ARCHETYPAL PSYCHIATRY AND GESTALT SWITCH
DESERT SOLITUDE ERA
BALANCING FORCES
CRAZY LOOSE CANNONS
PROSPERITY WHATEVER YOU DO
GLOGALISM UPDATES
CALLOUSED MONSTERS
BRINGING PEOPLE UNANNOUNCED
I'M SCARED OF THESE PEOPLE!
NARCISSISM IN YOUNG
LION'S DEN OF SNOWFLAKES
IT HURTS LOOKING BACK
NEED HEDGE OR HUSBAND

TRUTH ABOUT PEOPLE

WOMEN AND CONFORMIST CULTURES
TO BE UNIQUE BE STRONG
RATTLESNAKE IN YOUR CAGE
SUFFOCATING ADDICTIONS
SNOWFLAKES TRIGGERED BY DIET RULES
FATARIAN: IT'S ABOUT SATIETY
TRUST GOD IS THERE
YOU CAN DO IT GIRL
FALSE CHURCH
OLDIES ARE DEAD, YOUTH ARE WARPED
TWO LIVES: PREPARATION AND SUCCESS
THERE ARE NO MORE LADIES
IMMINENT DOOM
HOLY VACUITY: PROPHET IS ZERO
THE COMMUNIST SPIRIT
GRATING WITH THE UNIVERSE
NARCISSISTS ARE BORING
DUNNING-KRUGER EFFECT
BOUNDARIES AGAINST BOASTERS
EVIL HELPERS
PUBLIC PROCLOMATIONS
CREATIVITY COMES THROUGH
RESISTANCE TO GENIUS AND HOMEOSTASIS
SYSTEM MAINTAINS IT'S OWN LEVEL
NON-GENIUS IS SUPERFLUITY/NONESSENTIALITY
HIGH STATUS SADIST
UPSTART IDOLS LOSE APPLAUSE
HER FLYING MONEKYS HATE YOU
NEVER LOVE AN UNLOVER
WOMEN ARE MEDIOCRE THINKERS
DESTINY IS DIVINE
STRESS DEGRADES PERSONAL REALITY
SOCIAL ADAPTATION
EXPECT A TURNAROUND!
HUMAN RELATIONS BLOCK CREATIVITY
LIFE IS A PIE
HUMAN PARADOXES

TRUTH ABOUT PEOPLE

THE MIND IS A BATTLEFIELD
SEPARATE FROM LOSERS/BE A DESTINY-CRUISER
SOCIAL HYPNOTISM
WORDS COME FROM TRAGEDY
SEPARATE FOR SUCCESS
FAMILY/HOME AS FORTRESS OR STRESS?
OLD LADY DIET
T RUTH IS OPPOSITE TO WHAT WE'VE BEEN TOLD
NEVER BE ON THE BEGGING END (AGAIN)
LAST MINUTE TURNAROUNDS
PURE GOLD TRIED IN THE FIRE
PLANT SEED AND <u>WAIT</u> (TO BE DISCOVERED)
THEY CAN'T BE CRITICIZED
PRIVACY: AN INALIEANABLE RIGHT
SUDDEN OVERNIGHT SUCCESS
GOD KNOWS WHAT LIES AHEAD
SUDDEN HAPPINESS AND BEAUTY
AFTER TRIBULATION, FANTASTIC VACATION
ORIGINAL SYSTEM VS. MASS ATTRACTIONS
HARVEST IS RIPE: START TALKIN'
TURN IT ALL OFF: NOW HAVE HIGHER THOUGHTS
NOW LISTEN TO NO ONE
IGNORE MERE APPEARANCES AND CIRCUMSTANCES
WHEN POETS DIE
RELEASE OBSTRUCTION: SUCCESS
HOLOCAUST DENIAL IS HATE SPEECH
FREE SPEECH IS INCITEMENT
BEAUTY IS SELF-DISCIPLINE
BULIMIA KILLS
FAUNA-FASTING
DIGESTIVE ISSUES
MAGIC GLUCAGONS
FRUIT AND FAT
QUEEN OF THE FRUITS
DATE AND FRUIT SMOOTHIES
PORK IN THE POWERLESS
KEEP A LEDGER/NEVER FORGET
THE IMPORTANCE OF LEISURE

THE TRUTH ABOUT PEOPLE

COMMON SYMPTOMS MAKE CLEAR

Symptoms of their psychopathic narcissism becomes more clear as you learn common patterns.

When you see it in others and we exchange notes its an AH-HAH experience of insight/thought.

Your life's an open book in Borrego. The minute you get into town they're all gossiping you know.

There's trafficking then practically the same thing if you are unboundaried-- they own you see.

They rise up nonverbally and you get the feeling if you step out of bounds you'll surely be beaten.

When their nonverbal hubris is that evident you must mark it and nip it in the bud--get the sheriff.

The constant haranguing breaks you down. Their accusations become a program to do them.

THEY WEAR US DOWN

The constant arguing with enemy in my house broke down body and the immune system/ouch.
I
t breaks you down until others are sayin': what did he see in her anyway? There's no winnin'.

He'd accuse her of something. and she'd do it. It acts as a program to one who can't intuit.

Why take his side? Do you know what it's like married to a dam alcoholic--a Jekyll and Hyde?

THE TRUTH ABOUT PEOPLE

Anosognosia: It's the booze baby, not "him" but as an interactional disease the spouse is sickened.

If you don't learn from your parents you're gonna have to learn it from the world—far worse.

In California they all own you but in Utah it's self-governing, into their own thing, you're free.

Marriage is like a cocoon—you're protected from the mainstream and it's devices to deplume.

But if you've been dating you know what I mean—they can be mean cuz hatred is the scene.

Watch who you get involved with cuz your life can turn suddenly. Don't let em in & tell em boldly.

PETTY COMPETITIONS

The ruthless gossipping and petty competitions in a small liberal town: I'm a survivor, wow.

They incited riots against me, they came to my house. Always with an army of monkeys of course.

Sick family system always extends out. The sisters lay evil seeds and the system repeats itself.

The sister gossips on phone 100 miles away and it's enough to assemble the monkey army ok.

They come to your HOUSE. Americana is about privacy, this is wrong, more like anarchy or nihilists.

Once pegged they fill their cup and it's near impossible to change image 'til overwhelming evidence.

Little lady seems harmless, right? She is NOT. She has the power of the sheriff who she calls a LOT.

THE TRUTH ABOUT PEOPLE

She uses the sheriff as her right hand man to balance forces around her either men or women.

I felt like I'd entered a dark prison. The men wanted to use my body, women seethed with vermin.

The little harmless lady is balancing forces within her--that means to keep you down lady/sir.

SOCIAL WAS LIKE A PRISON

I felt like I'd entered a dark prison. The men wanted to use my body, women seethed with venom.

Angry pit vipers: that's how women seemed to me. They'd get on the horn & gossip incessantly.

That's how they rule domains: underhandedly, in secret meetings, on the phone manipulating.

No healthy calm debate just inciting riots against you. That's how the liberals and feminists rule.

Try living in a small liberal town where bad is good and good is bad, you'll see I'm right about fads.

I was so relieved to get outa social prison I felt He had risen again, like it was Easter or something.

Virtue signalling, social managing, power balancing, petty competing was not my mystic journey.

My mystic journey vs. virtue signalling, social managing, power balancing and their petty competing.

ESCAPING TO A GHOST TOWN

I literally had to escape to a ghost town to experience the solitude I craved, away from them.

THE TRUTH ABOUT PEOPLE

Churches were just as bad, thinking they own you and making you conform to their unique thing.

But it's a personal religion, I found that out all alone in a ghost town without you around/just the Son.

I'm not going to adapt to the Traditions of Men cuz they are the problem like the Pharisees before em.

The Traditions of Men are NOT the word of God, they are dusty relics and dead men's bones/flawed.

Jolly Jimmy will take it, take it & take it 'til he gets an edge then he'll come back with a vengeance.

If docile dad refused to do what she wanted it turned into a sudden barrage of hatred towards him.

MOM SAID "GIVE HIM THE BELT"

If mom isn't calling the sheriff she tells dad when he gets home: "give him the belt hon'"

The tough feminist uses men as her flying monkeys and she's always on the horn manipulating.

No narcissistic mothers? Think again. A few are nice but the majority are feminist harridans.

Passive aggressives are intent on domination but too dishonest to admit it so it's all hidden.

Democrats are the party of weak men and angry women so their only weapon is pass the buckism.

Their major weapon is deliberate obfuscation and they all do it with many words and confusion.

We can't allow angry mobs to make a country's laws. That's why things like lynching are outlawed.

THE TRUTH ABOUT PEOPLE

Women who are happily married but then seek even greener pastures have had it for sure.

ENTER WORLD SUCCESS

Success comes like a lightning strike. It hits at the right moment--that teaches us alot, aye?

You EXPLODE onto the scene. Wait for the right moment and never force the fit, just be.

Psychology is my field but words, phrases & picturestrips are the instruments of course.

Whenever it comes between doc or music choose the latter cuz it opens you up to infinity sir.

Poor countries recognize wisdom but in the west everyone is: the Dunning-Kruger effect.

Nothing happens for years--your dry period--then there's an event and it takes off quick.

Suddenly someone sees your potential and that's it, they sign you up for everything/it's God.

"What is this? I never heard anything like this, this is sensational!" That's what they'll say ya' know.

You go from having too much time on your hands to not enough time in the day: success/hurray.

For success, simply ask God for it. It's as simple as that about all other things--go for it.

THE TRUTH ABOUT PEOPLE

People: I can't stand em, you can have em. We're told to love God FIRST not be people-worshippin'.

THE TRUTH ABOUT PEOPLE

Man who loves her may treat her like crap when a lower archetype is evoked. If a queen, he won't.

HELL: Mental illness set in when she suddenly had to adapt to you and all your friends.

Trust your feelings and instincts. If things get too hard it's not of God and becomes a dam hex.

I invited YOU to stay on the land for a spell not your brother/lover/family and all your friends.

The fact you'd impose all those people on me without asking me or even THINKING how I'd be.

Your friends got vicious when I said I didn't want em around, that I just wanted to be alone.

She was so sweet but mental illness set in when she suddenly had to adapt to her step son.

Mental illness set in after meeting her step daughter [sister in law, etc] and to evil she caved in.

Mental illness set in going from sweet solitude to the pissing contest of immature girls/dudes.

Dealing with you for just a short time was like a tidal wave hit me and I'm totally exhausted, aye.

Retirement [age] means you do what you want when you want and don't take any more guff.

Three days adapting to you, three days convalescence getting my bearings back, what a nuisance.

ELDER CONSCIOUSNESS

As the body recedes the brain takes off to cosmic consciousness and this is elder bliss.

THE TRUTH ABOUT PEOPLE

As the body recedes the temporal lobes explode to reveal ETERNITY: this is elder sagacity.

When young I was strong enough to sustain the battles teaching me more than a library of books.

I could never endure it now: the mixed signals, identity struggles, treacheries of the unstable.

As the body recedes you get wiser in defining yourself in the world while blocking time-wasters.

The most important lesson I learned in life was BOUNDARIES because if I'm alone, it's victory.

Don't call em socialists, liberals, progressives etc. For the sake of brevity call em COMMUNISTS.

Women are group-oriented and it's the way they think: you're unique so they all become finks.

SMALL TOWN HIX/SOCIAL TRICKS

Suddenly the whole town turns against you instigated by an officious busybody: like a Nazi.

They had to conform so will make you conform and ruin your rep until you're totally torn down.

The group is crueler than the individual and as they take counsel together they feel so clever.

Older women beat up the younger ones in one way or another--these old bags are evil weather.

The most sadistic Nazi prison guards were women and this is very well documented about em.

Leftist Lunacy: Just as they defund the police they wanna take our guns for self-defense.

THE TRUTH ABOUT PEOPLE

He projected his angry violent father inside, an introjection that scared me besides.

Very few are self-aware enough to view their history and mine it for gems but that's the best.

True boundaries are endogonous [inside] but a narcissist's are contumacious: always a fight.

TRAUMATIZED BY CRIME

Traumatized by crime is a life-changing event. We hide/build walls not rely on government.

Studies show there's a contagion of lunacy in families and the result is exhaustion honey.

Women chase men now. To have sex with a man to hook him is witchcraft and beneath y'all.

Sex is expected on the first date in the degraded west. She's made to DEFEND chastity as best.

Few girls are verbal, self-aware or disciplined enough to say a definite "NO!" to expected sex.

She caves in when he calls her prude when that should be a trigger warning about the dude.

You slipped so now he says it's a contract. No way--just cuz you sinned don't keep it up honey.

TIME GOES ON, GENERATIONS PASS

The generations pass along with all memory with them, to be replaced by legends/their visions.

Time goes on, the generations pass on. Now they deal with their maker about all that went on.

THE TRUTH ABOUT PEOPLE

Those who scoffed at his humor or scorned the crown he served saw he was the best man for sure.

It's a matter of constraint of what you want to do. We're all born mad but some remain so too.

I'm an endless spout now. I can't even find time to fix food for myself, just a bar or nuts at desk.

Sometimes success only arrives by outliving family tyrants and other like serial bullies.

Outlive family bullies then it's YOUR season as all you touch prospers and thrives.

Everything is seasonal: the unforced patterns of nature. You're. down then up from below.

The Hero's Path contains a down, the best teacher around. Debunk then reconstruction.

HUMILIATION PRECEDES TRANSFORMATION

Utter humiliation and defeat precedes winning of the great. Keep going, escape bad fate.

Humiliation precedes transformation. It's the beginning like an initiation, endure it son.

As you spiral down everyone else turns against/tries to kill you too in the Fallen Hero Syndrome.

Instead of looking back in horror and remorse, realize your Waterloo taught you the most.

Anyone as different/talented as you they'll talk about, banding together against your loftiness.

The less intelligent the more they despise novelty and can't adapt. They just hate you man.

THE TRUTH ABOUT PEOPLE

Psychology doesn't talk about la la land/cumbaya but abnormal deviances, of course its negative!

"Don't be so negative, only listen to positive"--fine, don't study psychology of your relatives.

It is disgusting what is now expected of girls and you must build assertion in your daughters.

WIFE OF ALCOHOLIC SYNDROME

When he resumed his drinking career he became a frighteningly different husband to her.

When he resumed his drinking career he aged decades overnight and became an ogre/a fright.

When he picked alcohol up again he started calling his wife ugly and old, fat and a dam bore.

Since women see themselves in the eyes of others, she caves into this sudden change around her.

She may become alcoholic herself and raging. The system turns against her, not the husband.

Now she's lost her support system while Jolly Jimmy gets pity for being married to a harridan.

The dyads, triads and interlocking jealousy patterns come against her to finally do her in.

It spreads out in concentric circles until everyone in town hates her too--this is hell to a female.

Evil sisters encourages this with their constant gossip as past events are always brought up.

Always building coalitions against the one, the Odd Girl Out. It's really hard married to a drunk.

THE TRUTH ABOUT PEOPLE

The mere atom of alcohol puts him in the left brain and he loses holistic vision, a right brain thing.

The alcohol allergy induces GUILT which is blame-shifted to the wife who can't take it.

When the FOOL shows himself to be wise they all see it like hot coals are poured on their head.

A drunk ages ugly overnight so he's compelled to pull down his wife and the family's in strife.

Go to Al-Anon and generate even more gossip. I didn't like it and can't truly recommend it.

Al-Anon wives discuss their husbands in the meetings, a way of getting back or self-justifying.

Wife of Alcoholics: Release with love, release with hate, release that demon whatever it takes.

THEY STEAL PIECES OF YOU

People are now so vapid and cruel get involved with any one and you're up a creek/screwed.

There's an evil army all around and it's in my way. But I believe in Your promises, so I will wait.

It's not the end it's the BEGINNING of the end so stop saying you're old and look UP, be bold.

They tore her down so much she lost self for 30 years then slowly built back up by the Potter.

People strip you of your identity through their malicious gossiping, deriding, siding.

The woman's only weapon is getting on the horn again and telling all she knows by embellishin'.

THE TRUTH ABOUT PEOPLE

So that's all I gotta say: keep distance, maintain boundaries, get into your INNER reality.

Now I know it was just a dream. A beautiful completed family until you escaped to a new tree.

The only thing giving her solace was realizing it was a mental illness especially after all this.

The stress of being put down constantly and MISUNDERSTOOD did her in for good.

Eldering Sagacious: As the body recedes the brain takes off to cosmic consciousness: bliss.

MODERN SOCIETY IS LOGORRHAIC

It's just something I had to go through. The onion must be completely peeled back to the core.

"I hear voices yelling at me". Yes but you weren't in a concentration camp or prison: feel lucky.

Modern society is logorrheic: yak-yak-yak, on and on they go and where it stops no one knows.

She didn't do anything, her hands are clean. It's the people she incited against me you see.

The psychopath acts out and decompensates at the drop of a hat--resist, or reward that.

She's ashamed for her bad behavior but that's the Wife of the Alcoholic Syndrome, a bummer.

To end embarrassment or remorse separate your who from you do--it was a demon not you.

It's ok to be arrogant and grandiose if your motives are good & you've done your Great Works.

THE TRUTH ABOUT PEOPLE

Never let em tell you who you should fear or not. That's plain evil--it's your instincts or rot.

She told me not to fear her boys, I accepted what she said then they ruined everything friend.

FEMALECENTRIC FALSE CHURCHES

The Churches: Since women got control they're not preaching the true gospel that's all I know.

Husband's duty: to make his wife mentally well. Many are crazy at first then things go swell.

Systems Patterns/examples: 85% of the daughters of dual alcoholic parents become bulimic.

All she must do is take control of the situation she's in but instead she escapes to worse bedlam.

With marriage there's a growing war between her virtue signaling and his logical thinking.

Does she succumb to her husband's natural conservatism or does he give in to liberalism?

I contend most husbands are going along with their wives just to keep peace at any price.

On the woman's side is much confirmation from main news, her friends, the culture at large.

If husband stands his ground there's gonna be a war and she may even label him dangerous.

With disagreements she gets on the horn and her friends side with her against the monster.

MEN CAVE INTO LIBERAL WIVES

THE TRUTH ABOUT PEOPLE

Few modern men are alpha-male strong enough to go against their socially-grounded wives.

Since her mother and sisters are liberals, she has support systems everywhere against the male.

Culture, media and society agrees with her and there's growing hatred for his views for sure.

Imagine a growing frustration in the male as this is occurring--few are ready for what's coming.

Long story short, he's labeled paranoid psychotic with mandatory drugging as guns are taken.

Long story short, it ends in divorce and he can't see his kids again and he's banned from everything.

Husband talks of globalism and his wife panics like he's a nut then gets on the horn to vent alot.

Men are meant to protect/provide and that's conservative but wives push em to the left.

Self-forgiveness is easier by seeing it's a mental illness. We get sick then there's wellness.

Having gone thru all that now you're stronger to avoid mental illness and instead be alert/fit.

ALL DEPARTMENTS FEMALECENTRIC

All departments/legal systems are now femalecentric and that's the end of freedom I think.

It's usually trauma that starts the mental illness, something stuck and festering I guess.

You gotta work thru trauma and complete the mourning cycle or it creates later trouble.

THE TRUTH ABOUT PEOPLE

I battled the Dunning-Kruger effect for thirty years and it taught me more than a library of books.

Happy husbands live ten years longer than unhappy or single men, just that proves what God said.

Modern society is social hebephrenic: word salad, mixed signals, trivia, attention getting.

The psychopath doesn't have ego-control mechanisms he just acts out the id: basic functions.

Go to hell you little demon that's what I shoulda said to em but instead I caved in, to a dungeon.

You don't need a sign cuz you know what God said. He promised you prosperity in your season lad.

When you're good to people they want more and when super-good they want more/more/more.

An era of mental illness reflects in disordered people in the mix. Put it ALL in a bag then dismiss.

I'm only happy behind a locked gate knowing it's gonna be a GREAT day cuz it's just my fate.

Evil Stepmother Archetype: They were compelled to bring me down, they wanted their mom.

I was so relieved to bear visible fruits because before then they saw nothing/called me nothing.

CALUMNY AND SOUL MURDER

She tore his family apart & ruined his rep. It's called calumny--soul murder, whether true or not.

She tore you down whenever anyone was around. She's a calumnious soul murderer hon'.

THE TRUTH ABOUT PEOPLE

With their **WORDS** they incited people against you and **THEY** were the violent ones: RENEW.

When we die all these bonds and bad memories are null and void--of non effect, vaporized.

With their **WORDS** they incited people violently against you so God holds them responsible too.

Petty crimes--broken windows/public urination--aren't prosecuted now so it **ALL** comes down.

Prosecution of petty crimes keeps **BIG** crimes away so letting them go is destroying the country.

They **WANT** bedlam so they can take it all over with globalism so they ignore petty vandalism.

Happening all across America: they aren't arresting petty crimes. Trash everywhere/culture dying.

The extreme status-tension and aggression with females drives em to suicide/homicide.

PSYCHOPATHS ARE ABOUT BASIC FUNCTIONS

ID: Eat, drink, sex, sleep: like a shifting strobe light that's all he is--overwhelming/no boundaries.

No fear or rejection like the emotional borderline, just alert hunting for and securing his supply.

Instead of looking back in panic over how close you came to disaster, thank the Master.

I eat a cheese omelet every 48-60 hours with just juice/water in between. Pedro, your fan.

It was like being in jail with those people or a rattlesnake in my cell but I learned very well.

THE TRUTH ABOUT PEOPLE

It wasn't so much you they hated/resisted but the archetype evoked by your behavior sis.

Joyce Meyers was raped 250 times by the age of ten by her own father. Feel grateful sisters.

REPENTANCE RAISES ARCHETYPE *WAY* UP

Repent your behavior, change/uplevel your archetype and the past dissolves just like that.

The psychopath meets an eventual void from insisting on remaining shallow: drugs/sex/food.

Narcissists can be very interesting but psychopaths never are, they're boring in shallowness.

Repetitive, trite, they spew cliches all night. They're shallow and boring forever all right?

Sexting on first chat shows severe mental health issues and no matter who they are, eschew.

73% of all divorces are initiated by women bringing their own house down. How dumb.

Mortification: when the false self crumbles and grandiosity can't shield him at all.

Studies have shown that all people LIE 90% of the time about everything--how funny.

I was working a false identity to get ahead quickly and it all imploded one day--terrifyingly.

Parents: eternally grateful I led em to heaven and that compensates for all my trouble, amen.

Narcissistic mortification: when the false self crumbles and grandiosity can't shield him now.

THE TRUTH ABOUT PEOPLE

The false identity buttresses up self for a time despite constant anxiety of the worst kind.

SUFFERING & OVEREXCITABILITY = GROWTH

Yes I'm a psychologist Ph.D. but it's my SUFFERING that makes a poet an ocean of emotion.

I had to make gold on early trauma & be re-made on the potter's wheel to be here as me now.

I had to overcome crutches developed thru the years to endure an infinity of emotions/fears.

You have the trauma locked in, the anxiety resulting and the false identity just for living.

Let God make you an endless spout too. Repent of all such coping devices [sins] old and new.

People are cruel so your early lessons are how to overcome the herd in your house.

You're trapped under the same roof with someone playing cruel games, driving you crazy.

The minute they have you the cruel games start up. You're at their mercy cuz you took a chance.

He seemed nice "live here, for just light housework"--soon after he became to a sadistic jerk.

Don't ever move in unless your name's on the deed. Burn your bridges then beg on your knees.

He seemed nice "live here, for just light housework" and later he became a sadistic jerk.

You gotta stay in control, HERE, in your power base. NEVER, EVER give that away to an ass.

THE TRUTH ABOUT PEOPLE

Students are afraid to express their opinions because of the other students, not the teachers.

The peer group pressure is enormous, imposing, officious and violent. Even now I remember it.

Self-forgiveness is crucial but difficult for success--it helps to see it all as a demon I confess.

After her mother put her down constantly/publicly another spirit took over like a monster.

ARCHETYPAL PSYCHIATRY AND GESTALT SWITCH

This is archetypal psychiatry. They can't see both sides of the template simultaneously.

Don't ever let em in and **NEVER** get in a car with em. I've been tyrannized especially by women.

There is trauma and a new, lower archetype intervenes and it's like another person, very freaky.

We live in an age of lost civility & violence. You must stay in your houses/avoid homelessness.

Four hours I had to endure being in the car with a bully and that taught me everything honey.

DESERT SOLITUDE ERA

Lived in a tiny dusty cabin on 1000 acres for decades and learned to love every minute ok?

I sidestepped all the cultural changes that way and when I came back new they hated me.

When I marched to a different drummer after solitude in the desert they saw me as a sinner.

THE TRUTH ABOUT PEOPLE

The extreme status-tension and aggression in females is deadening, frightening, aggravating.

When two girls meet they size each other up, compare, sabotage, ridicule, enjoy gossiping too.

The female community is like the old west. You gotta learn how to traverse it to stay blessed.

Getting drunk herself is the main reaction of the wife of the alcoholic, in fact she's called it.

Anger comes out while drunk and all feel sorry for the alcoholic being married to such a skunk.

Jealousy is written in DNA of the modern feminist. So far removed from her best she just hates.

I've written it all down now what happened before i had protection, a husband and a home.

BALANCING FORCES

Balancing forces while remaining untargeted trying to get ahead despite my constant dread.

Living under the same roof with a dam alcoholic and my spiteful rude stepchildren: yuk!

Living under the same roof with spiteful sisters joining with my foes in sick jealousy triangles.

Living in a small liberal town with people dropping in unannounced wasting my time: ouch!

Living with a husband with nobody else around giving each other SPACE to study: PARADISE.

Constantly balancing forces soaked in adrenalin trying to control what they're thinkin'/plannin'.

THE TRUTH ABOUT PEOPLE

Being alone with a husband in a lovely home with no one else around: this is highest heaven.

Female community is a giant obstruction to her genius: she can't trust either sex, that's how it is.

We all have our Waterloo, the path is down then up for the hero, I was far down as one can go.

Best leaders were victimized first. How. else could I learn about people, the best and the worst?

Stats show happily married men live ten years longer than unhappy-- divorced/widowed/single.

Men love to ridicule the sins of women while forgetting their own accepted-as- normal sins.

Women are getting promiscuous thinking it's male freedom when it's lost beauty and doom.

As things degenerate trust turns to hate. Hire someone for work and they rob you ok?

CRAZY LOOSE CANNONS

She's crazy but can't see it. Caveat: having her around is a loose cannon/I can't take it.

As a member of a modern cum-bay-ya church she was sad, empty, scared, bored--yet an elder.

The SPLIT starts with early trauma. Something unacceptable to the ego by those who love ya.

I couldn't stand having here here. Loquacity and drip-dry hangers with empty lives and beer.

I splashed into the desert after divorce and other loss. The women descended on me, jealous.

THE TRUTH ABOUT PEOPLE

I had depersonalized--forgot who I was--so was an easy target for women and the envious.

Undercut and override, undercut and override. That's all I got from you broads and the snide.

If one is sexually promiscuous or they're comin' onto you sis reject the mess and be blessed.

I was terrified of the little demons. Tring to be their friend just egged em on. 20 years I caved in.

Give me a sign, I need a sign. Adulterous generation seeketh only signs and have no spine.

PROSPERITY WHATEVER YOU DO

God said whatever you do will prosper as all your fruits come out in your SEASON, and it's comin'.

Suddenly all my fruits came out in 130 segments just as God said, like a harvest as I was led.

People are cruel and if they think you're lower/a nothing the results are brutal and real.

I want you to be a someone cuz everyone has something, a rare talent/new art maybe.

When I graduated I thought I knew it all but the real education came later in the human jungle.

They create dystopia on purpose because they enjoy stomping on us and it always gets worse.

Criticize AOC--hurt her little feelings--and cops came to the. door. This is serious I declare.

GLOGALISM UPDATES

THE TRUTH ABOUT PEOPLE

When you wake up all you want is protection. Not things, clothes, trinkets but life to go on.

When they get the upper hand it's like you walk into a torture chamber with no one to help.

The new movies are gory and violent--they both reflect culture and create it so we must separate.

New movies are violent, woke and sexually deviant [as if it's normal] and I'd say to avoid it.

Maybe it isn't workaholism. Maybe it's just interesting to em or gives them an identity friend.

If one's self-image is grandiose he must have the works to buttress that or no-deal Mack.

It's ok to be arrogant and grandiose if your motives are good and you've done the Great Work.

Those people scared me half to death and you brought em here. Now I see you clear, bye dear.

They were garish and nervy, officious and flirty, overly affectionate and didn't even know me.

We create thru *subtraction* not addition. We create thru *elimination* not accumulation.

CALLOUSED MONSTERS

They were calloused monsters. Wherever they went they created disaster: car rollovers etc.

The frenemy worms his way in then hangs: a drip-dry hanger. Then he tells all about the owner.

I can still hear people yelling at me, loud voices. Now I'm sure it's the snowflakes/nuisances.

THE TRUTH ABOUT PEOPLE

Wherever they went they created inevitable mistakes and anyone involved rejects the flakes.

I pity the parents of these monsters esp now being broke they're moving back in the house.

They were snippy dishonoring brats, always getting drunk and inviting all their friends/rats.

When with these types you'll experience a homesick feeling of dread and depression, oh man.

What you're sadly homesick for is your SELF which is being ECLIPSED by someone else.

BRINGING PEOPLE UNANNOUNCED

I am horrified by those monsters you brought to my house. Can't you tell a grifter/lush/louse?

Only your frenemies come unannounced with an army. This is invasion, oh how you dishonor me.

They were "triggered" when I said you shouldn't snack between meals. What is this, snowflakes?

The frenemy will worm his way into your household then gossip--he's a leak to the streets.

Stay away from these people, block them out/don't talk about, forget they ever existed, resume work.

I'M SCARED OF THESE PEOPLE!

I'm scared to death of these people, get em outa my house, now: that was my life, unbelievable.

I'm scared to death of these people, get em outa my house--that was my life up to now.

THE TRUTH ABOUT PEOPLE

Wicked men holding captive weak women in their own **HOUSES**: There, the bible says it.

An extremely smart person such as yourself oughta really make it big--I'm talkin' renowned.

What holds us from that, our destiny? Other people! Think of it, left to yourself you'd be ok.

God doesn't want you constantly in fear, drying your bones. He wants you to be victorious.

I'm not gonna sit there & argue with creeps like that. It's circular, slippery, never-ending, futile.

Giving up useless debate is like opening a gate to your gorgeous new mansion and estate.

They are violent--we are losing civil society--so sorry I must isolate to find any serenity, truly.

He acted nice at first, a cute kid. Then asked me for drug money threatening like he's gonna hit.

If they're gonna act like that they'd also kill you without thinking about it. Era: **UNEMPATHIC.**

My one fear is ending dependent on em at the end of my life. For this I rely on Jesus Christ.

NARCISSISM IN YOUNG

After time with a narcissist you're worn out and feel like a shell of the person you used to be.

A narcissist's self-absorbed controlling ways show no sense of reciprocity and that's your reality.

The snowflake culture has seriously embedded eating disorder groups-- disgusted with all rules.

THE TRUTH ABOUT PEOPLE

When I said "no snacks between meals" they reacted with disgust saying how triggered they feel.

I can't deal with these undisciplined brats so contumacious even in innocent chats.

"No snacks between meals" was interpreted as "bloody murder" to the teen people.

Instead of getting to know each other slowly they send pics of their genitals immediately.

Self-discipline is always an answer and fruit of the spirit, but just the words and they hate it.

LION'S DEN OF SNOWFLAKES

I don't know if I can go back in the lion's den with them--they insult, mock/ridicule/condemn.

There's no more civility and they've been trained to disdain people like you and me see.

I don't need to be mocked and ridiculed like that, ever again. You dishonor me and I'm gone.

Arrogant/obnoxious/contumacious snowflakes act like they need to have their face slapped.

They need boot camp but it scares me to say that cuz that's what they want for us the brats.

A couple tablespoons of nutbutter and I'm sated for three days. Amazing start to fast ok.

They are so cruel and callous I'd hate to see what they're like in their personal lives.

There are 60,000 quips going into this work, I'm not surprised I made a couple bad remarks.

THE TRUTH ABOUT PEOPLE

If they flew paper airplanes at me in the 70's imagine what they'd do now the snowflakes.

Seeing violence/pugnacity as an answer to everything: they'll burn down your house honey.

Our war is from within and where are all the real men?   All the while the borders are wide open.

It's awful disgusting looking back. For all us cuz we swam in muddy waters: face it/forget it.

You're to be a lightning rod to your generation but this can't be done if you're one of em hon'.

It was the sixties when alpha males were lovers being very influenced by the crooners.

IT HURTS LOOKING BACK

I'm so embarrassed because now I'm a lady and looking back makes me wanna escape into a hole.

She wasn't a slut she just had porous boundaries with no self-awareness and wanted love sis.

She'd get drunk and go wild with repressed trauma "coming up". It was a horror to witness.

Started getting drunk at 15, started puking at 24. What came first in A. A.: Alcoholic Anorexia?

She coulda died so many times & you made it so much worse by hating her guts for that rut.

Years of trauma showed on her body so later her new hubby gave money for plastic surgery: ok.

Was it you who stole my pen? I don't care if it was just a pen that's what I'm talking about friend.

THE TRUTH ABOUT PEOPLE

NEED HEDGE OR HUSBAND

Without a hedge, a husband or firmly laid boundaries a woman is targeted quickly honey.

Even without her mal-adaptive coping devices [SINS] they woulda hated her, that's just it.

Look back not to feel remorse but to mine the pearls from seeing everything in reverse.

The only way to be safely unique is through repentance. Then you're bold, not defenseless.

Moral unsurety incites opposition and until your back is up you're increasingly degraded man.

You're partly there as a red pill man but not all the way--you still sin or go along with the women.

You're a red pill girl but not enough backbone in boundary-assertion: YOU incite em.

If you've broken away partly but not all, you're a weird and limp handshake and will surely fall.

WOMEN AND CONFORMIST CULTURES

Weaponized immigration flooding in so we're all just an atom then we're taken over globally as ONE.

The universities show a general antipathy to Western civilization so ANY other nation is better.

Women from conformist cultures will HATE the odd girl just because she didn't/couldn't adapt.

Odd women sent to concentration camps, delivered up by neighbors and their long dossiers.

THE TRUTH ABOUT PEOPLE

Never get in car with a woman like that, she'll drag you over coals while she has you captive.

It's cuz she's different, but not just that. She must be strong enough to BE it without flack.

I was in her car when she turned and attacked me like a barking dog. Then nice again, huh.

The minute she has an edge she'll abuse her authority over you and that's it, you're dead.

If she gets power/control by withholding your pet she'll do that. Never let on what you want.

The Jezebel let go on me like a barking vicious dog then expected me to forget it all, huh.

TO BE UNIQUE BE STRONG

If weak they'll attack those differences but if you're strong they'll go to your conferences.

As you look back you see how close you were to disaster but finally saved by the Master.

To be victim of someone's shitty personality like that--demons out of the collective unconscious.

NEVER be at anyone's mercy. Don't even take a chance it may happen, forever and eternity.

No matter how nice they seem, man has two sides: when they get an edge a tiger comes out.

If they have control and you truckle it's trouble. Never lose independence, make that double.

A boy with a mother like that grows up hating women not realizing it's the liberals/feminists.

THE TRUTH ABOUT PEOPLE

The inability to handle power while grasping for it in underhanded ways, managing images.

I burned my bridges and moved in. He showed his true self within a minute and I saw I was sunk.

Never burn your bridges cuz then you're vulnerable. Watch that power dynamic, make it equal.

To be at someone's mercy automatically puts you in the inferior category of the unQueenly.

The guy doesn't even have the right to talk to you/lick your shoes but here you're giving ALL.

He flatters her/she invites him in for good. He pulls her down/she begs him to stay/he's gone.

RATTLESNAKE IN YOUR CAGE

It was like putting a rattlesnake in my cage. To be a victim of a tyrant's personality and rage.

She was a great hostess and cook but got drunk bi-weekly then our home life really sucked.

I can't have her as a friend again since it's dangerous how she belittles me to her friends.

Control through social networking: always on the horn, working it. Balancing forces, getting back.

Germans found women made the best prison guards. They were meanest with most disregard.

It's all about power of the powerless. They need victims to play that out, dumbed lasses.

The odd girl out--the peculiarly unique--draws ire from the female crowd, ever mocking and loud.

THE TRUTH ABOUT PEOPLE

As soon as that creepy weak guy gets you he'll abuse his power, discard, change his view.

PTSD: Praying constantly for God's protection when there is [no current threat] protection.

Don't go back to previous stations and relations cuz things are never the same son.

They put you down [degrading your self-esteem] to cover their act and you just took it on.

They laid an evil script on you [they lied] and you acted it out perfectly, proving them right.

They laid an evil program on your identity and you like a sad child acted out your self-treachery.

When the victim went back home she walked into a wasp's nest of jealously hostile relatives.

Once the grapevine took off like that her reputation was sunk & nothing she could do about it.

SUFFOCATING ADDICTIONS

When I couldn't get drunk I'd eat and when I couldn't eat I'd get drunk. I'd say that's a trauma bond.

It's like the crutch is holding back a tidal wave. In most cases we need a good long cry then ok.

Did mom give your dog away without asking? Stuff like that causes trauma then later addicting.

26 years in the desert wilderness in a small cabin separated me as culture marched me by.

Sometimes submission [to the Lord] looks like DEFIANCE to those who conform.

THE TRUTH ABOUT PEOPLE

Your willingness to defend yourself will always trump your ability so draw boundaries now.

You can love someone and not wanna be with them or even ever see them again, amen.

I'm a catalyst in discussion groups until I leave the group in a huff when misunderstood.

SNOWFLAKES TRIGGERED BY DIET RULES

The snowflakes yelled bloody murder when I said no snacks between meals/they hate rules.

I call it Spoon Theory: take a tab. of nut butter then that's a dense meal to weather the fast.

For those of you who don't wanna wear your dentures may I suggest creamy cashew butter.

After a cheese omelet I fasted 48 hours, now filled with power. Where do I go from here? Pedro

High fat diet is far lower in quantity but raises total load on immunity so you fast longer see.

I love the niftiness of a little nut butter replacing two meals, spoon theory makes life easier.

Eat a cheese omelet any size then you fast 48 hours and handsome Pedro says it's the best.

If you're into all those grains and fiber, enjoy it. I'm sick of gut aches, high fat smoothes right in.

I'm sick of having to fix all that food and those dishes. I don't even wanna go into the kitchen.

We fast longer between meals to compensate for raised load on immunity: it's a budget see.

THE TRUTH ABOUT PEOPLE

High-carb dieters eat many meals but sages/elders don't wanna eat all day, that's how I feel.

I got tired of looking for something to eat when all I needed for satiety was a piece of cheese.

Arts. of Paleo Fasting. Animal, nut, fruit, veg. Omelet one day, fish feast the next, nutbutter if less.

FATARIAN: IT'S ABOUT SATIETY

FATARIAN: It's all about satiety cuz with high-carb hunger felt like nausea but now, no pain.

It's all about satiety--whatever gets the job done so we can do our thing. Fat's most efficient see.

It's a burden: should I have rice, noodles, potatoes, crackers instead? With fat I feel well fed.

Whatever releases me time, energy and work brings **ENLIGHTENMENT** cuz life's a budget.

And when you consider how much time and energy goes into our food life, it's a real high.

TRUST GOD IS THERE

God turns plans of nations to naught and an effectual prayer of **ONE** is all it takes for that.

Never use circumstance as an excuse for cowardice. Come in boldly and He will show up sis.

There is none mightier than You. No government oppressing it's people is pleasing in Your eyes.

Forgiveness isn't saying one is wrong and one is right but a release of burden/illusion of control.

FALSE CHURCH

THE TRUTH ABOUT PEOPLE

Churches will be the main pushers of evil cuz they're not churches just enemy outposts.

The satanic energy I feel in these churches is worse than Los Angeles itself. Alex Jones

That awful feeling of loneliness and emptiness being in Los Angeles will be worldwide as globalists.

I've fought the good fight, I wrote what You told me to write. Separation from God is my fright.

It's called SIEGE: the oldest form of warfare is to isolate by turning off energy, food, water.

They're here to help, they're here to help--all the while his speech is blood-curdling evil.

Stop calling it a "hypercritical" spirit when in reality and truth it's a spirit of DISCERNMENT.

OLDIES ARE DEAD, YOUTH ARE WARPED

You gotta see persecution as a reaction to your sins, otherwise you will feel like a total victim.

Oldies are. dead, the youth are gone or warped, no one remembers anything about this ol' girl.

Suddenly my fortunes changed and everyone's against me. In one second it's all uprooted: tragedy.

I want to enjoy life every minute and have a beautiful place to do it--that's all I know or care to intuit.

I don't want "him" I want a relationship and if "him" is worthy and willing he'll compete for it.

Take your focus off the man and put it on the relationship you want or you'll be WAY up, WAY down.

THE TRUTH ABOUT PEOPLE

Having skill sets for relationship are ultra-important for who wants to be alone and protect himself?

Relationship isn't 1 + 1 = 2 but 20,000 to infinity. With you & me it's an enriched environment [EE].

You MUST go no-contact or you're forever on the begging end--that's hell on your self-esteem friend.

I had to produce or die: that is, be labeled as crazy, lazy or delusions of grandeur insanity.

YOU CAN DO IT GIRL

Sister said I had delusions of grandeur--the one thing she learned in school-- not "you can do it girl".

New life will be wonderful compared to the old life which was miserable overcoming the rabble.

What Dunning-Kruger put me thru adapting to dumb would fill a library on Social Psych, 130 volumes.

It was frightening knowing they didn't and couldn't understand me knowing how they saw me.

In fear of being misunderstood and rejected from the pack you settled for less, a dam sad sack.

The Lord vindicated me, saving me from strife and confusion. I still remember the awful feelings.

Things were rarely flowing in synchrony, I was usually grating with everybody before maturity.

It got to where I HAD to produce or die. Something they could finally see and be totally ashamed by.

TWO LIVES: PREPARATION AND SUCCESS

THE TRUTH ABOUT PEOPLE

There are two lives: preparation [overcoming/talent developing] then total world renowned success.

The first life was horrible adapting to heathen who felt superior seeing me as a despicable person.

I was dying--the light diminishing--then called to Jesus who brought me back with this Creative Act.

One can only mal-adapt to the liberal environment of petty competition and sterile dynasties.

To be put in that matrix and compete on that basis literally made me sick, becoming as bad as it gets.

To be accepted I had to agree with the family opinion leader cuz she was older/went to Stanford.

But she was fullabull and disgustingly wrong, a dangerous influence, a soul murderer and gossiper.

I had to produce or die at the hands of dumbed down, underhanded and vicious female foes.

You've planted a helluva seed, the Creative Act is complete. I'm humbled, what an incredible thing.

THERE ARE NO MORE LADIES

They are no more "little ladies" but angry trendies not above pugnacity and anything nasty.

Why compete on their basis/turf when you're on your way to another world? Be above the little turds.

Women were so jealous they dripped with it. Ever colluding/planning but God saw the bagashits.

In divorce women will do anything to ruin their EX for life with vicious slander and endless strife.

THE TRUTH ABOUT PEOPLE

Calumny has lasting effects on the personality: by always trying to compensate we can't create.

All I did was defend myself against the witch. Her constant snipes made me wanna be rich.

Immoral: If you disagree you're a moral lesser, there's wrong in you, you're a phobe and a hater.

Leftist authoritarianism is becoming more dominant every day in America, ramping up under Obama.

Husbands: How can you believe her when you own eyes say it isn't true--stop listening to The View.

It's so disgusting how you look at your wife before speaking--she knows nothing you weakling.

IMMINENT DOOM

I was scared every minute being a drunk. That was a toxic reaction cuz inside I knew the hedge was down.

A feeling of imminent doom cuz inside I knew I had lost all protection if the crutches were of Satan.

Only dependency on God and repenting of sin--coping devices to fit in--would bring me home again.

It's never fun being a sinner. It is terrifying, socially destroying, body-depleting and mind warping.

Stop worrying. God's punishments are over, you repented. Need to relax so keep this central.

HOLY VACUITY: PROPHET IS ZERO

It's a prophetic process: you empty yourself, go out into the desert, holy vacuity, zero = prophet.

THE TRUTH ABOUT PEOPLE

In one instant he sees how puny he is in the scheme of things--the most important pivot I think.

Americans are big individualists but in collective we'll be absorbed into a huge glob/total abyss.

Suddenly we're surrounded by strangers who don't respect our customs or our dogs/cats.

Suddenly we're absorbed up into the mass, the cold heartless narrative of images and lies.

That's what you are going along with liberal narratives/globalism cuz it's communism hon'.

It really wasn't your fault you just believed a lie. A lie which took you down to hell instantly.

Send him an innocent pic or meme to let him know the job is open then disappear or it's a bad omen.

Rib-breaking hilarious comedy which is suggestive is the most thoroughly culture-degrading.

The communist spirit: you have more than me so I'm gonna bring you down and make you pay.

Just cuz I'm gonna be gone sooner doesn't make me inferior but that's how they think in fear.

THE COMMUNIST SPIRIT

Communist spirit: you have two kittens so give me one. NO, I got em together as family/get your own.

The communist spirit is imposing, it invades your home looking all around/asking to borrow some.

I felt the communist spirit even entering kindergarten. I hated being around peers, I friended older ones.

THE TRUTH ABOUT PEOPLE

Ever smiling [cheese] in photos. It's the social subset of the communist spirit--we're to be communal.

She smiles cheesecake at everyone--how phony. Bearing teeth is a sign of aggression too--the irony.

There's a book called The Borrowers and that's the communist spirit: don't allow it sisters.

It's confusing to lend stuff out--a mental hazard. I have it all for a reason, the rest I give out.

I have stuff cuz I want it here and when no longer useful it goes to another so stop borrowing sister.

As a tortured artist writing is such a a pleasure--being so pissed off it relieves all the pressure.

GRATING WITH THE UNIVERSE

Grating with the universe was a consequence of sin but now things will be flowing/you'll be in.

The verbal abuser drops bombs then insists you forget it. If you rattle his cage about it you'll regret it.

Two choices: Relapse into their system (be neurotic) of be yourself and never see them again.

Due to sin/world, man's eyes lose their shine, skin takes on a grime and they all say "he's no friend of mine".

I'm doing it, found my groove. You're reading it and will improve.

From clutter to clarity, chaos to orderly: Happens momentarily--a click in the brain then we're happy.

It's highly embarrassing and disconcerting to meet a powerful performer who's in reality immature.

THE TRUTH ABOUT PEOPLE

Just be sweet, be yourself, stay simple. No need to play these phony roles with personality crippled.

I'm done, not just a bum living in a cabin anymore, it's a mansion.

It's so much easier to be alone as the magic elf. Otherwise you spend all your time explaining yourself.

Looking back it was the rejection which came first THEN the mal-adaptive/bizarre psych syndromes.

NARCISSISTS ARE BORING

Her sisters rejected/superiorized over her first THEN she became a psychotic addicted gypsy anarchist.

She felt fiery arrows of envy/hatred/suspicion from women but after marriage they were instantly gone.

They were sadistic. Upon deciding you are a targeted class they make life hell for you very fast.

Listening to him is like a very unsatisfying meal. He's so shallow you want more but it remains nil.

He just doesn't get it or embellishes non-truths or things that are irrelevant. You can't fake IQ man.

DUNNING-KRUGER EFFECT

It's the Dunning-Kruger Effect: a dummy thinking he's smart and Lording it over his followers/idiots.

Giving advice over petty things yet totally missing the main points of morality and all it's underpinnings.

Marriage is freedom for a woman. The feminists have it all wrong--it's our only defense against the throng.

Listening to a shallow one who thinks he's really something leaves us wanting because he's so empty darling.

THE TRUTH ABOUT PEOPLE

We wanna be filled but there's no wisdom there--an empty bucket with holes. He's missing and he's dull.

You've learned about clouds without rain--human disappointments--well he's just empty man.

The worst is when a Dunning-Kruger imposes on you. Guard against this so there's no downer effect too.

Dumb either want what you have, impose their will somehow or bore you for hours like a bovine cow.

BOUNDARIES AGAINST BOASTERS

You gotta lay boundaries constantly and enforce them or be run over again by these envious interlopers.

And you don't let em in your house--that's where they can do the worst abuse, with you without defense.

They're too dumb to restrain acquisitive desires, they just want a piece of you and act like it too.

Like Jews in Nazi Germany the perpetrators accuse em of things that are absurd/groundless--expect this.

We must work to protect targeted groups--including those who are just different being attacked too.

I was attacked by both sexes for being different. But the youth got violent about it--think about this.

They lurch at me like they want a piece of me. I never wanna be with them again, I want liberty.

They want things from me/don't know how to treat me. Just that would take study, it's all about history.

The lady said "first mom put me down publicly but when the sisters took over I collapsed into insanity".

THE TRUTH ABOUT PEOPLE

They will turn against you if their friends don't like you or get their friends against you: POOH.

EVIL HELPERS

Under the guise of "helping" you they just bring you down and make you a clown to all around.

Under the guise of "helping" you they're sitting in your lovely house as an evil leak to the street.

I am so sick of the non-issues you ascribe to and your embellishment of many things irrelevant too.

I feel a HUNGER after listening to you cuz you're a DROUGHT of real meat in a meal.

Borrego was an emotional drought and I thought I would die from wanting real true relationships.

An evil helper will make ten times more work for you and ruin your reputation too. To chaos bid adieu.

The question is who's the teacher here. At first I thought it was you but now there's nothing I wanna hear.

PUBLIC PROCLOMATIONS

My dear the things you say in public, on youtube or to an audience! I'd watch it bud, it jumps out at us.

If things jump out at them--even if just one word--they'll think about it/ruminate over it and reject him.

Stop remorsing over an immature past. Remember it was the Queen's Disease and it certainly didn't last.

Why debase an entire culture by what you say? Why lower the tone, why help em slide into hell today?

THE TRUTH ABOUT PEOPLE

What I hear is constant name-dropping/self-adulating and so you're in for a downward spiral buddy.

It's like you don't know any better/your parents never taught you anything and it's embarrassing.

A genius knows how fast he can lose success so each move is planned and he doesn't take chances.

While drowning I called out for Jesus tho' I didn't know Him and He brought me back with a Creative Act.

Strive for perfection and every day practice. You know what you wanna do, act as though you have it.

CREATIVITY COMES THROUGH

He's "coming up with" stuff. True creativity comes from God and we know it-- it satisfies/not empty fluff.

Does your mother approve of how you talk? Are you just trying to get approval of younger folk?

Talking about genitals/sex acts--it's gross cuz swimming in muddy waters has dulled your conscience.

If you're just "coming up with" stuff it'll be DRY, DRY, DRY. Only stuff coming from God is clever and high.

Not everyone thinks about sex constantly like you buddy. Some are decent, think about that or die.

It's like an adolescent desiring to shock. Everything he does is for a reaction but you're an old adult!

Don't say you're the Renaissance man, BE the Renaissance Man. You're all about image, not God's plan.

Look what happens when men are not leading women: Kids are sexualized when they should be playin'

THE TRUTH ABOUT PEOPLE

Once women get the upper hand they never let it go. It's crucial to an unstable identity: being in control.

Male power is perfect love, female "power' is virtue signaling, tyranny and reversing everything.

Males don't want their sons turned into females--this stuff is coming from women towards their children.

HIGH STATUS SADIST

His cruelty knows no bounds, he's a dam sadist. Anyone close to him knows this yet he's high status.

The weak female will do anything to hold you back. If identity depends on you being down, she'll react.

If she hates dad but dad loved you mom persecutes you too--mothers vs. daughters gets very cruel.

If dad loved you more mom keeps you down and makes sure by gossiping about your every quirk.

Mother had to **PUBLICLY** humiliate her daughter since her exiled husband always loved her more.

If dad loved you more and you started to excel mom was quick to take you outa your lessons doll.

It's not only the evil mother but the evil sisters--they all chime in together against the one so clever.

What do you think Greek tragedies are all about--FAMILIES and their dramas, wars, killings, treacheries.

You hear the pseudo-mutual side of families but rarely how they hold down genius/the anomalies.

Who are we closest to? Our families so there's the dialectic of disharmony when sin strikes.

THE TRUTH ABOUT PEOPLE

UPSTART IDOLS LOSE APPLAUSE

The upstart immature idol will self-implode as talkers start to notice things and withdraw applause.

In standing up for the wrong thing she got real drunk and MADE them listen, ending up in an institution.

It's aristocratic to have LESS not more furniture. Stop stuffing your rooms to see more of the wood floors sir.

The worst housekeepers won't let the poor little pets in but the best ones let em in and love them.

Worst possible thing is be on the begging end. It sickens him--he'll kick you out fast if you act like that.

Bulimic tendency to jettison with tension and it's genetic but the relief from obstruction is rewarding.

It's not her it's the evil spirit making a home in her. But nevertheless you'll turn against her, yes sir.

Feminists are vindictive towards men. "I'm gonna bring him down" they say and to cruelty there is no end.

Most female cruelty is getting their flying monkeys against you and it's an army. Relentless frenemies.

HER FLYING MONEKYS HATE YOU

You make a new friend, all her friends hate you. Either she mocked you or it's a sick system blocking new.

The narcissist keeps only foolish flatterers around. Any genuine critics he bans for life and beyond.

A big family is great but it fills time. For those of you alone hold that thought for you're free to really climb.

THE TRUTH ABOUT PEOPLE

I see life and each day as a pie. Because I put destiny first I just don't have time for you--no offense, bye.

He was just a chump then the vids exploded and his ego took off but still too immature to grow up.

I'm ready to let you go, you're just too shallow. Life is a pie and this keeps me from the really valuable.

I'll admit I was initially enamored with you but then human foibles showed a fool/you busted my rules.

NEVER LOVE AN UNLOVER

"Me, love a man who doesn't want me? NO WAY." Quote by the First Lady of the United States

No I'm not a woman-hater, I'm a woman sir--it's the feminist thing in her, a loathsome evil mocker.

You can't fake style buddy. Unless it comes from the heart--inborn or won--you're just a dull copy.

Play it cool if you want--we've always been taught to do that--but keep in mind you may lose out.

Stop fishin' on the net and study your pets. Get offa this thing and attend to your own situation I said.

Oprah said when young she was a slut and didn't know it, a result of no ego boundaries--can you see it?

Tho' it started about childcare, new feminism is the reverse of everything femininity is and it's really a scare.

Now I go off to my destiny as an old lady surging with vitality/seething with vituperative originality.

I'm not going there anymore, I get bored. You gotta come here if we're ever gonna soar/confront the horde.

THE TRUTH ABOUT PEOPLE

I'm afraid you're gonna get me off point or start thinking wrong [carnally]--how you shit-shot the ladies.

I'm thru going there or anywhere. It's all in here from now on and every minute is important to a seer.

I'm not wasting any more time with you. Life's too short and every minute counts as I endlessly pursue.

WOMEN ARE MEDIOCRE THINKERS

Women are mediocre thinkers: statistics show. Some get beyond it but unfortunately most don't.

If a public speaker better have your shit together cuz it'll come out--all that stuff hidden you figured.

A dry season indicates a coming Tsunami--it's always empty before mass attractions overwhelm thee.

Why tie the knot? If a woman is alone she is targeted but if she's married she is not.

Nazis: The most effective propaganda is a grain of truth encompassed in compelling hyperbole.

He would be someone who [once he's deflated] would just be hanging around and hold you down.

Your obsession with another has warped your soul, stolen your time, misdirected your energies--let it go.

DESTINY IS DIVINE

You have a divine destiny as well as a divine design to each moment but he has muddied that phenomenon.

How good you'll feel when this black cloud has passed. For that's what it was, dark/empty lowness.

THE TRUTH ABOUT PEOPLE

Never let em push your pace. Cuz then you start making decisions based on what THEY want, ok?

They're setting you up to obey. Don't let em lock you down for their comfort, truckling to what they say.

Don't ever let em push your pace so that you're uncomfortable--slow down or leave it all.

If he persists on the quickening and in exhaustion you give up the boundary then you'll be hurt honey.

Remember: Pushing your pace is for their comfort and agenda, not yours--slow down or get hurt.

Don't care about another's feelings more than your own, for they use em to manipulate you--just stay home.

Your home is your kingdom of comforts/defense then suddenly you're thrown in with others, homeless.

STRESS DEGRADES PERSONAL REALITY

God stop this slippery slope--give us reason to hope! With these things happening how can we cope?

With stress people fall into their bag. That's everything from envying to being a drag or loving to brag.

Now is the time to hold on to personal reality. Despite all, this is your only serenity and serendipity.

All we can do is pray. But that's the most powerful remedy and just one needs to do it, okay?

At noon, I'm off. For life is two-speeds: Action, and reception. Active-relax, perception is freed.

In all your hobbies and projects, be neat and orderly. That's important to true genius/a mess isn't funny.

THE TRUTH ABOUT PEOPLE

My Donald's gonna call me, I know he is. I don't know why but he's my guy and we'll discuss all of this.

Though the sky is falling all you have is what's in front of you. Just live this day and God will protect you.

Forgiveness releases able-bodied mentally fit workers to do your bidding, excited to be contributing.

When you pray it tells God you want interaction: giving you discernment then energy for action.

Women with goals should choose husbands who are God-loving, hard-working, honest and loyal.

Maybe only age gives you discernment and if that's true, what a retirement.

Great performance by the lady but her interviews belie total insanity.

Acting out emotions to resolve inner issues.

SOCIAL ADAPTATION

Here for now, tomorrow forever gone. Out out brief candle. Shakespeare

As a psychologist I study humans in relation to their systems and the moral is: keep your distance.

The unrecognized genius has not learned to be alone: In truckling to trends he remains unknown.

God empowers you for battle--to have class. This gives control over all from the low to the brass.

The would-be genius follows trends. In trying to please his friends he misses the unique gems.

To be a world success, don't need approval. To bring out your core, social neediness needs removal.

Those aren't friends--you have nothing in common. You just see being alone as

THE TRUTH ABOUT PEOPLE

rotten (hitting bottom).

In social generations, solitude is seen as hideous. How stupid--no wonder non-creativity is insidious.

Genius avoids trends--the herd matrix. He just does his own thing and becomes rich and famous.

Early sins can later do us in. It's a time bomb on the body waiting to happen--but with God begin again.

When the scapegoat rises up, she flourishes. Then, those who held her down sink and swim with the fishes.

Nothing feels so good as a turnaround back from the brink. The past was just learning from the stink.

EXPECT A TURNAROUND!

When adapting to them I felt like a Harley-Davidson bogging way down when it's meant to go full speed on.

The devil made you do it because you went where angels fear to tread then you made your own bed.

Oh the feeling of going beyond a persistent problem--to transcend and overcome after hitting bottom!

My uncle's passed to the other side. This has been a psychic opening and sparked me from on high.

The family can be the best institution or it can be the worst (i.e. not caring: you don't come first).

A dog is not just an object. Make arrangements for him in the event of...

The sick family is drunk with power. As it implodes the scapegoat rises up: man or woman of the hour.

The same weakness is in those who held her down. Imagine that--after they told those lies all over town!

THE TRUTH ABOUT PEOPLE

They can't keep you down forever! For all those years of suffering now you'll accomplish your endeavors.

Was it your sister who told those lies? Was that your brother who ignored your cries? Open your eyes!

HUMAN RELATIONS BLOCK CREATIVITY

Human relations mess with your mind. High IQ means you see all levels and most of it's not kind.

Once you hit on a key point, keep milking it. Let it simmer all day and night as it evokes thought.

When the nice guy lies to you, even a little, see him as just another maniac and be noncommittal.

On the net there are echo chambers of nonsensicalness so please go/leave me be or I'm joyless.

I suffer, I write.
People get depressed/suicidal in social isolation but it's an opportunity to find the true self/ELATION.

How much painful rejection is really ageism we don't know but just live your own life anyhow.

Stop trying to recapture past. Even if you went back it's never the same, God is eternity not old games.

I had to work through so much outer chaos to get to the core but once I did it was automatic: whoa!

No man knows my history so why tell em stay a mystery

Must clear away the outer dross: crap from culture, old wounds, sick relationships, failures.

RESISTANCE TO GENIUS AND HOMEOSTASIS

THE TRUTH ABOUT PEOPLE

If what you're doing is totally revolutionary it may be that everyone will hate you: it's your jubilee.

Find your predestined groove, it's the highest point and holy spirit smooth so repent, I behoove.

Just give up on them, they will never see. Don't waste one more moment and enjoy being free.

The sick family hates the best and brightest of the bunch. Some may have to see that before their launch.

To the sick family, good is called "bad" and bad is called "good": The "bad" is an angel and the "angel" a hood.

SYSTEM MAINTAINS IT'S OWN LEVEL

It's homeostasis: the system maintains it's level whether good or bad. Stay separate, no more sad.

It may hurt being alone but if you persevere the pain disappears and soon your genius star is shone.

In the sick family one becomes the angel and the other the devil. Then they switch positions (never level).

The sick family is the basis for addictions and psychosis--as water seeks it's own level, it's a symbiosis.

When the victim recovers but goes back to the system, he becomes sick again--that is my wisdom.

If the victim gets well and doesn't get sick, another member implodes (just as sure as the clock ticks).

I hereby declare to switch reality from outer to inner, including my family and friends--a real cleanse.

Doing things his way he got a bad rep. That's the way of the hep but it'd be far worse staying in step.

THE TRUTH ABOUT PEOPLE

It hurts being shunned, hon'. It's a common reason for suicide so hold your head up high--you've won!

NON-GENIUS IS SUPERFLUITY/NONESSENTIALITY

Non-genius is marked by superfluity and non-essentiality. A real bore can't streamline to the core.

They're heartless because the heart is blunted in this world. Educate their heart: find their pearl.

It's not their fault, it's how they're taught. They're under a social hypnotic trance in lies they bought.

They're dead wrong but don't hate them for it--they just haven't been told. That's your function and it's gold.

Shunning is sh*t. It's such a common thing with evil children or neurotic adults I had to do a quip.

Can they get any more phony? Must they fawn/gush for approval from their cronies? Hah: baloney.

Some women are trite, shallow, carnal and willful (un-cheerful) and when they talk you get an earful.

Music's the fastest therapy as it opens windows in your mind--your scene. TV is the opposite: all fiends.

TV and internet--so much static warping your mind. You may not know it but just music is such a find.

Don't recall embarrassing incidents, put it all in one bag: the devil. God forgives it all, you're level.

Your work was suffering, your suffering was work. After all that refinement you retire into the perks.

Find what works then do it daily. The answer isn't perfection--just look distinguished, not plainly.

THE TRUTH ABOUT PEOPLE

LIFE IS A PIE

Life is a pie, man. Do you want so much of that in your plan? Release emptiness, open new span.

Caution: Do you go along with group attitudes? That's your ruin as your genius sinks to platitudes.

Since life's a pie just decide what's important and to the rest say goodbye then fly as you apply.

Peace at any price: You think they'll let up--but soon their insults are back up, your dreams blown up.

Don't give yourself over to them. Use restraint and pull back to your own sphere--don't be a suckup man.

Old systems call you guilty 4 past sins 4 which you're forgiven. They want you down: shame-driven.

Life's a pie--the more you spend here, the more not-there. This stops the waste which brings despair.

There comes a minute when you give up for good. Life changes suddenly after killing that big bug.

When you conquer fears (of aloneness) they'll call you a seer. Having cut the BS you're in full gear.

I've always strived for meaning. To me it meant instant healing--it always stopped the heart from bleeding.

If you're great they bash you, If inventive they sass you but If you conform they'll still trash you.

Like I told you, life is a pie. When deciding what to focus on in the moment: see the pie, say bye-bye.

To do your best work, take the day off. The clearer you get the easier the completion: blastoff!

THE TRUTH ABOUT PEOPLE

I'm not a hater. I describe the psych--of the lesser to the greater--and how the latter's from the Creator.

Tired? Persevere. Alone? God is near. Sad? Have good cheer. Mad? Open to new happy frontiers!

Start your day well-informed, be a student of life so they be warned, avoid the rabble or be harmed.

This life is just a shabby porch to a magnificent mansion--so look ahead and endure all treason.

HUMAN PARADOXES

Human paradox: the "nicest" are (in truth) the meanest: facades creates conflict and then weakness.

It's easy to be complex but hard to be simple. Simplicity is a mark of maturity after the messes/pimples.

It's hard to be simple but easy to be complex. When I try to read all that I'm left perplexed--bad effects.

The mark of a genius is how many people DON'T come back at first--for if not best he's the worst.

Prudence sees the trouble that's coming and hides itself. The sinner says "it's all okay"--not a magic elf.

For them to get their's, first you gotta separate the wheat from the tares--the good from the bears.

Due to demons our tangents were absurd. We lost our way, lines became blurred--forget, now gird.

Divide from the mutts--mind your gut! For it tells all and if you don't listen you'll end in a rut with no out.

These are mean helpers. They'll do anything to get you hooked to drugs, downers or uppers.

THE TRUTH ABOUT PEOPLE

Enemies have plotted against and hunted you like prey--it's hard to accept when it's your own family.

Whenever I feel shame I think of the cross. No matter what I did, because of what he did, I'm boss.

God doesn't want you belittled so stop those crazy thoughts: your social knots create blind spots.

Think of the cross whenever you feel shame. Let it settle all doubts that now you're not to blame.

THE MIND IS A BATTLEFIELD

The mind is a battlefield, so keep the bad out as you remember the cross settles all doubts.

Don't worry, for the fake are flimsy. But that's also why in their friendship there's so much treachery.

Can they get any more shallow? No, and when it comes to moral courage they're just plain yellow.

The enemy has plotted against and hunted you like prey. That's hard to accept when it's your own family.

"The tables are turning": Keep saying that, come outa your sleep, start learning and then earning.

Guard your mind by substituting thoughts. When you think of them replace with the cross.

People get old, age and die but the traumas they caused still remain in our brain and that's PAIN.

Get some class, hick! Draw lines and be sturdy--strong as a brick and split from the thick, quick.

It is possible that marriage takes us the rest of the way--struggling for years but this saves the day.

THE TRUTH ABOUT PEOPLE

You just gotta meet the one who'll make it all happen. Then He takes over while you enjoy nappin'

He's a cute kid but inside a creep without character. The latter takes decades if they lacked a father.

She came to awareness fifty years after the original trauma. Neurosis can last decades, or not.

Childhood emotional neglect causes isolation and distancing later. Despite help they feel they don't matter.

SEPARATE FROM LOSERS/BE A DESTINY-CRUISER

Separate from losers and destiny blasts open. These are the blind, the walking dead and the unchosen.

Psychosomatic illness from porous ego boundaries--you let the scoundrels in, thus bad association is sin.

Trust no man--that's what the bible says. Just love the Lord not fragile humans though they be fans.

The genius has few friends that he can trust. To the world it's a hideous thing that we can't thus adjust.

Watch who you put your faith in, friend. That's the most important thing I leave you with--now transcend.

Once you let these creeps go your destiny blows wide open--your new show for those in the know!

I got hurt--that's why I talk like this. I learned my lesson well after they used me only to dismiss.

What is true grit? It's more about separation than physical strength--can you draw lines, can you split?

When you think of them do you get a stomach ache? That's your solar plexus warning to stay away.

THE TRUTH ABOUT PEOPLE

To be Truth you go against the grain. I know the resistances to genius, the urge to conform--but no gain.

SOCIAL HYPNOTISM

You're way ahead of your time and that's why they mock and degrade you, the pathbreaker sublime.

If you're a genius people call you "fickle". You're multi-talented so you want it all--not just a trickle.

It's bad to be captive to another's projection. This is mind rape you must escape though it means rejection.

Protect yourself from hurt by not trusting those you shouldn't. Look at track records not listen to pundits.

I was broken by society and had to build back up. God put me on the potter's wheel with growth nonstop.

When you see their true colors, don't forget it. Don't let it drop unconscious as usual only to repeat it.

Once you see traitors recall back to all the things you submerged. Make a list of how they scourged.

No matter what's happening, creativity will keep you high. It's God comin' through--to the world bye bye.

To get ahead you must reject false idols. These are people you thought were great but now no-nos.

You gotta do your own thing--not look at what others are doing but just sprout in your own stream.

The function of poetry is to be so simple they can't dispute it and that's why I love it: don't reason, just intuit.

I suffer, I write. I suffer, I write. And it's been this way for forty years, day and night (high as a kite).

THE TRUTH ABOUT PEOPLE

WORDS COME FROM TRAGEDY

The words came from tragedy and emotional tumult but then was rewarded with big bux in the wallet.

Turn it off (what tracks the mind) and the environment comes alive: your destiny illuminates, no jive.

Music opens us up (wide) as TV closes us down (narrow) and that's why it's music or be fallow.

Dogs/cats love music cuz it's mathematical. That shows what's best for us too--be right-brain fanatical.

Our pets want music, not all this crap. To them it's just chaos and noise they'd like you to scrap.

Be kind to animals--turn the TV off. Your pets just want music not this other stuff--it makes life rough.

Compared to the chaos of TV noise, music opens mental windows inciting famous creativity and poise.

I finally turned the TV off for good. It's not just the crappy programs but me not thinking like I should.

Thank you God, you made me see the detriment of TV and then you gave me something better: me.

Your write the draft one thousand times then the final one: higher poetic images. That's the most refined riches.

I scribble words from my heart-pain and if it hits a vein and you know it, that's the function of the poet.

SEPARATE FOR SUCCESS

God gave me another chance, He brought me back from the dead. He told me how to live and be fed.

Rather than posting how much they hurt you, just delete em--that's the

THE TRUTH ABOUT PEOPLE

simplest way to defeat em.

To innovate you gotta think out of the box. That means not lookin at what they do--that only blocks.

Keep locking the whole into place, that's all you gotta do. The rest just takes care of itself, for it's the truth.

God said that all is vanity (emptiness, falsity and futility). This godly viewpoint has great utility.

She is so pat, so phony, so obviously insecure and just out for the money but she calls you honey.

I don't know what it was--bitterness or brokenness--but what a mess. Waiting on God gave me finesse.

Goodness in the present rectifies the past. Try it: invite past foes back in your mind and have a blast.

FAMILY/HOME AS FORTRESS OR STRESS?

Divorcees think it's normal: their broken relationships. It's not--it's rot--but they are told to endure this.

Marriage is coming within walls. There is no greater high when this battle is won as our destiny calls.

The un-family becomes obdurate: obdurately against you and especially your views and it gets worse, too.

The body responds first (panic) then the frontal cortex reads what it "means": the brain is a fishy scene.

The un-family are blockheads: more like a fable and when it comes to meeting your needs, less able.

The self-sabotaged cleave to the un-family for results which never happen, amen. Find real friends.

THE TRUTH ABOUT PEOPLE

We see moral insanity looking back. We all had a little as we absorbed culture and the fickle or the simple.

Un-family victims feel guilt and shame but when aware and separated these feelings are tamed.

The un-family makes you want death but when released you become stealth as God injects new breath.

The "loving" temptress hurts many (wives) women. Don't get too close or you'll be treated like vermin.

Men need marriage too, though they go to lengths to deny it. They suffer with divorce, so better to accept it.

Marriage is coming within walls, for it's scary out there. Both sexes need it or life's too much to bare.

Be what they want you to be. You disappointed before when they needed you more so now stay up--see?

OLD LADY DIET

The mark of genius is how many people don't come back. Most all want gross entertainment--fact.

For you to get the benefits first you gotta admit that you're an Old Lady. Are you pushing 50? That's nifty.

In the Old Lady Diet our only exercise is maintaining house and a garden. Against all intruders, harden.

You don't take any crap on the Old Lady Diet. You just tell the truth until they can no more deny it.

I gotta write what I feel. That's all that comes up, a great deal--the current circumstance or a new meal.

Though the theory remained intact, after my stroke I could not adapt--when they'd say things, I couldn't track.

THE TRUTH ABOUT PEOPLE

Why do I need to constantly compare myself to others? That was facebook tension--underneath, it smothers.

The whole reason we got sick was adapting to them. With them on top our realities went black, amen?

They enjoyed excluding me--I was shunned. But now I've overcome all and that means a huge fund.

With death all these problems are resolved. After upset, hurt and mental damage you're God's pal.

TRUTH IS OPPOSITE TO WHAT WE'VE BEEN TOLD

The truth is opposite to all we've been told: resolving these contradictions is making gold.

The truth's said simply. Simplicity shows guts and self-assurance vs. wimpy wordiness and complexity.

When depressed I don't elect music. I must mitigate against this tendency and instead put on my therapy.

The best thing about eldering is the lucid recall of past pearls: we must mine these memories so our dreams unfurl.

Trendy man's too lazy to shave but the real man does it daily: he's the true rave (it's handsome vs. cave).

Our wrongness evokes their spitefulness and all other negative human characteristics: creeps and finks.

If they annoy you, re-focus on your own reality: Block them out, don't get caught up and fill thy cup.

No TV: Enter the delicious nothingness where the True Self's trying to get through despite our fickleness.

The solution is to shut up and wait: if your mouth causes problems be mute and don't take the bait.

THE TRUTH ABOUT PEOPLE

Being a man isn't strutting around acting tough, but doing the right thing even when things get rough.

It's about who's superior to who. Encrypted in the brain, like having the flu and pure obstruction to you.

Face the void which fear keeps hidden through addiction: It's your predilection and answer to all problems.

When on top you'll be protected from the herd but until then you won't be preferred and may be slurred.

It's not about looks: pin-up pages. It's what you stand for (lest you stand for nothing) bringing high wages.

NEVER BE ON THE BEGGING END (AGAIN)

Seeing the system releases resentments: See how you brought it on, a raving witch from a fawn.

They want you on the begging end (not your friends) and once you trust them they'll do it again.

Don't get caught up: in weird useless tangents, sucked into drama and other human derangements.

Mining: Separate out the false from the true, common from the rare (just a few) and it's about you.

Only God decides when we retire--when we stop: On the date of the last curtain no one's ever certain.

What is freedom: staying free of anything tracking our mind or blocking our destiny--that is liberty.

The only way to stay sane at this point is to ignore the left's silly statements: just relax (smoke a joint).

Was she my mad mother or older sister? Whatever, she was my worst enemy but I overcame the bother.

THE TRUTH ABOUT PEOPLE

Only her death erased the memories: of being put down, gossiped about with rep destroyed (calumny).

Things are gonna ramp up like you can't believe in the next several weeks-- hang on to your seats!

Can't go back so may as well go forward. Old regrets (though we repented) turns us to salt: wrinkled.

Late-blooming adolescence is just as much an existential crisis.

Her constant criticisms drove me to perfection (in frustration) so I am grateful cuz now I'm on vacation.

LAST MINUTE TURNAROUNDS

Just when they said you'd never be healed, God brought a turnaround and you're the best in your field.

God turns things around so fast it leaves you speechless. He takes you so high your joy is ceaseless.

When God shows up He fixes things you've been struggling with for years. Instantly, gone are your tears.

God loves seeing you fight the good fight, rejoicing and praising even when pricked by the knife.

Realize the devil's the adversary--and that good's always opposed in an evil world, so be wary.

God-filled, you're a nuclear weapon! The past is wiped out and you make your mark though a brat or felon.

All that was stolen returns to you a hundredfold. Everything you lost will be coming back gold.

If obedient you'll eat the good of the land. He'll give you favor: more blessings than you can stand.

THE TRUTH ABOUT PEOPLE

You've been in the ditch but God's turning it around. Look at your enemies: they've all backed down.

God's getting ready to move on your behalf—so much that even silly friends or family will join your staff!

Now it's a divine reversal as all obstacles are removed. Your time has come, after years unmoved.

Troubles were a stepping stone, overcoming made you tired to the bone but now your star is shone.

PURE GOLD TRIED IN THE FIRE

Pure gold was tried in the fire. Being falsely accused has made it hard to aspire, but that was prior!

If it's important, say it. If it's not, shut up! Silly or useless utterances block thought you nuts.

To do something great you gotta deal with backbiters but that's okay, just concentrate on followers.

You've too much to give to not come out of this. Destined to be great you must suffer before bliss.

You've said bad things but God has cancelled them: You get the glory while evil is condemned, amen.

No matter what you did, it's not over. Just get closure then spring to grand life with a chauffeur.

You wait, wait, wait and suddenly it all happens: As your destiny blasts open so do your options.

It took years/decades to get to this point. Hard work paid off with wreck-aids which God did anoint.

Don't look at the misery you endured to get here. It was all just resistance and will now disappear.

THE TRUTH ABOUT PEOPLE

God said "what I need from you is thought: open your mind by cutting out all lies you bought."

We all have a shadow but sometimes others peg us for it when we're really in the light, though sorrowed.

The old are afraid of danger. They've lived, they know of the stranger and the money-changer.

Solitude is enabled by each other. For being alone seems the highest thing to us birds of a feather.

Maybe today is the day when future breaks from dreary past and you're a world success, at last!

PLANT SEED AND <u>WAIT </u>(TO BE DISCOVERED)

Think of it as an atom bomb or a seed you've planted, not a perfectionist document, forget all that.

People give you a funeral even though you didn't die. They agree to shun or it's outa the group, bye-bye.

If sensitive the most important thing is boundaries. This psychic armoring is also for memories.

The enemy seeks to traumatize and trouble you, but that's God's cue to move in, right on queue.

The enemy takes advantage of weaknesses, so you must stay sober and alert like all great geniuses.

God made us all unique. When we hide that (fear of disapproval) we cut off parts of self: a freak.

We all have two sides. It's a package deal--nice but a tiger inside. Prepare for their flip flops then decide.

What enemy meant for bad God turns around now. Their assignment is cancelled: you're in the dough.

THE TRUTH ABOUT PEOPLE

We must choose our battles: is it really worth it? Don't waste energy needlessly: they can't force it.

They're making fun of me: pray. Their talking against me: pray. God comes and saves the day: pray.

Weeping may endure for a night but then joy everlasting. Joy unspeakable and full of glory: blessing!

Success isn't from east or west but God who puts one up and the other down: you're renowned.

THEY CAN'T BE CRITICIZED

Just cuz you want things done right they accuse you of criticizing people-- aren't humans evil?

Get your head out of social drama/trauma and back into your work. No more shame only fame.

The success system: They don't believe you'll ever make it so give up on them/get new friends:

See worn-out relations as past shells of your old selves. Not applicable--it's dusty archives vs. new cells.

How can he love you when he can't love? Asking a legless man to run a race, yet you're a sweet dove?

Don't think whatever falls into your head. For Satan drops things in there and you'll dread instead.

They stabbed you in the back, gave you a funeral and forgot you—until now you've come back: new.

God uses the shunned misfits to shame the "wise", bringing them down to their proper size.

Get away from false teachers for untruths are exploding everywhere. Prophesy: avoid the snare!

THE TRUTH ABOUT PEOPLE

Families disown every day. That's when the head has it all his way until another has the say.

They hated her first--then the form that hatred took (in her) was horrible and hate-able: a curse.

God chooses the shamed sinners to confound the wise--for with repentance their true destiny will arise.

PRIVACY: AN INALIEANABLE RIGHT

There is no freedom without privacy. To interrupt one's home life (come without calling) is pure piracy.

He saved me from my enemy's sword. He brought me out of the chaotic hoard to freedom, restored.

They lied on you: It wasn't about you it was a demon from past actions creating hostile factions.

The most dangerous place is a thrift store: thousands of pieces of clothing all washed with detergent before.

Stop being an adjunct to another's thing. You've got your own--but are you seen as an underling?

In controlling her image she loses all reality. Since she's at the center, she's a dangerous enemy.

They were haughty, stiff-necked and bossy. You told God Almighty then He made you the head: cocky.

Always hoping things will change keeps you from grief's final acceptance, so bid good riddance.

Don't go to their pages, it kills you. They walked you by, they can't fill you. Withdraw to self: God loves you.

Pray to God because I tell you truthfully: few people will ever care about you, to speak frankly.

THE TRUTH ABOUT PEOPLE

Go to Jesus first off. That sets the path so you choose wisely/avoid those who scoff.

Present actions change the past and future. Einstein said there is no past-- now is the suture.

All of a sudden, you're rich. It's like it came out of nowhere, though you worked and overcame the witch.

It's a new season, a new hour of power which changes how you look: from a snail to a flower.

At times nothing works to get connection. Then a slight change of direction = perfection.

They can't do what they need to do cuz they don't have what they used to have: be free/cut sin in half.

SUDDEN OVERNIGHT SUCCESS

I should've lost my mind but there's a story behind: I had to overcome to take the job assigned.

If you've sown in tears (been through hell) it's so exciting to know your victory is coming, so let out a yell!

It's not about where you are but where you're going. Hold on, if down now soon you'll be glowing.

It's been a long wait but things are ready to turnaround: Blessings abound, you'll be simply spellbound!

Be weak because His strength is made perfect then. Worry and sickness will prove His greatness, amen!

They said you'd never be back cuz you couldn't have survived all that but God gave you a castle from a shack.

You'll say "look what the Lord hath done". Up to here life's been no fun but now the enemy's overrun.

THE TRUTH ABOUT PEOPLE

God's hedge of protection is about mean words--ricocheted off you and back to them in thirds.

He'll turn it around, okay? You've been prey but now God's done the impossible creating a brand new day.

God has brought you to a turning point. Now you'll have the last laugh, never again to disappoint.

I may have fallen down, I may have made a mistake. But God's my Champion-- He killed that lying snake.

Thank you God for taking my TV out. I'll not get another, I can take a hint--and I have no doubts.

GOD KNOWS WHAT LIES AHEAD

God knows what lies ahead so He gives you info making you dread: good, that's how we're fed.

The instruction may seem illogical: it won't make sense to your mind, until later God lifts the blinds.

They die but their spirit lives on (in all you think and do) whereas you never thought of them before, hon'

TV's on the blink and this acted like a shrink. At first dismayed as if driven to the brink, soon I felt in the pink.

Now it's just music and walking in the sun. These fulfill my retirement life: entirely homespun.

Now that I don't turn the TV on, my desert life has opened to a mysterious adventure: what fun!

Utter purity is blinding to the eyes. That's the effect of no obstruction which is sin in disguise.

What is strength? Freedom from obstruction. That's why repentance makes you superhuman.

THE TRUTH ABOUT PEOPLE

You reach a point where it's just clutter in the brain. Music dilutes the news horrors without refrain.

DROP OLD RUTS, NEVER LOOK BACK

While a broken pot I smoked pot and cried a lot. With God I dropped ruts and never looked back like Lot.

You can take so much of the left-brain, then you gotta switch. That wordless (right) space is so rich.

God has chosen that moment when your life splits into the future, free of the past (what a contrast!)

Suddenly you're rich, no longer poor. Suddenly your popular, no longer a bore: joy and grandeur.

All you must do is wait and work--then work and wait--until that moment of your Grand Estate.

I was in a dark bubble with decades of trouble but now I'm paid back double because I read my bible.

Don't you understand there's nothing to do but pray? We can't control this but we can enjoy our day.

A DEAD DRY BRICK, BLOCKED

You're blocked, a dead dry brick. Then suddenly you click and everything you do is so slick!

It happened to me. I worked and waited until the very end when God's timing was my best friend.

Suddenly you shift into higher realms. Then life reverses: either into success or it overwhelms.

A simple change of view and what was lost is now found. Looking larger, the implications are profound.

THE TRUTH ABOUT PEOPLE

What can flip a man's switch: wanting her so bad he converts back to reason "she's not a witch".

Hoarders need counselors to deal with affection for stuff. Just put it all in storage, that's enough.

Stuff keeping you down: Give away or put in storage, carefully labeled and now no more obstruction.

Creativity is: Seeing the ghost then filling in the DOTS. It's not from anyone else--you're the boss.

SUDDEN HAPPINESS AND BEAUTY

Great changes can happen overnight. That's your right as a child of God: outa the blight, into the light.

The power of poets is greater than an atom bomb on culture cuz less is more, inside they already know it.

Superior Man realizes once he's reached his peak he will only decline--it's ok as long as I can wine and dine.

You get better and better then you die. Not falter at the end but increase: be your best/reach your apex.

As things get weirder each day, the saints return to realilty where things are nice, decent, expert, high-pay.

Terse verse: laconic and wise. Cuz down deep we all know the truth about what we should despise.

Stop faking high self-esteem. It distorts the personality in anger and it's not being on the beam.

It takes what it takes. Creativity must expand to contract, so the road to greatness is often being flakes.

Much of what you went through was punishment for sin. Now you've repented, you'll have such joy again!

THE TRUTH ABOUT PEOPLE

To live in cosmic space (your genius) you must clear the mind and let anything that tracks it behind.

We all have something we do best. Do it, reach your crest by cutting obstruction, sins confessed.

See your greatest faux pas as just a blink in eternal space--nothing. You've magnified it to something.

With each painful recall the event magnifies in memory but it means nothing in eternity--we're free.

And few remember it anyway, they're too busy in their own drama/feelings of envy, jealousy, dismay.

Don't belabor past sins or feel persistent remorse because that's an insult to Jesus who erased it all.

Keep smashing toxic blocks by comparing to eternity, let the latter smother the flames/blast it out, be free.

When belittled we bow over, then we isolate (can't get closer). Solution: to prior systems get closure.

I think it's great they reversed themselves [on the wall] but so much damage was done. Pres. Trump

AFTER TRIBULATION, FANTASTIC VACATION

All drama is human-conceived. In death it loses relevance as if it never happened and we were never peeved.

After a stressful period of adaptation our eyes go out to the horizon. What a relief catching the energy thief.

In the whole family you were the only one chosen and that's why you have these visions and aversions.

Finally rid of detractors--your lifelong foes--the whole universe explodes in beauty: How it glows!

THE TRUTH ABOUT PEOPLE

Retire--into total leisure. To create your own heaven, it helps to see the world as an evil creature.

Maybe I'm gonna fall flat on my face as a true scientist goes by instincts not what the herd thinks.

We should all be a throwback to the greatest our ancestry shows. But if in sin, we reveal the dark and lows.

There's a destiny God lays out if we choose His plan. But if in sin you take the devil's track, man.

AVOID BAD ASSOCIATIONS

Why would you even call her? Don't you know what happens with bad association? Lure

That you would go to someone like that--the mere contact--is such an evil fact: so inexact.

Especially when your robotic "groove" relates to survival, it can become disgustingly psychotic with no rival.

It feels so good: freedom after the painful control. I'm joyous as everything realigns with new goals.

You picked the wrong person to mess with cuz I got God protecting me. Wait a little while, you'll agree.

Prepare: When you change all your interactions will feel it and they can turn violent, but stay vibrant.

They hurt me so much--not knowing what they're doing, that's my hunch (humans are a dense bunch).

ORIGINAL SYSTEM VS. MASS ATTRACTIONS

The war is in the psych created by the original system. These are templates which either rule or GO, amen.

Stop being a drug addict cuz you and some doctor clicked: he's getting

THE TRUTH ABOUT PEOPLE

kickbacks so he won't restrict.

God has set his anointed apart for Himself and He also gives distinction to this magic elf.

You've worked, waited, planted the seed and humbled "me": good actions bringing mass attractions.

He's the God of infinite chances--it is finished anyway. No matter how many times--you're okay!

Picture yourself on a long road with God. It's a giant destiny leaving behind those seeing you as "odd".

Jealousy triggers sick creeps. Though all around, stand strong: clean sweep, they're up a creek.

It seems like you wait forever--every day's the same. Then suddenly breakthrough--riches and fame.

Though 10,000 are against you (thought squad) recall they're flawed. The only answer to clods is to love God.

When I get too crazy (frenetic) I must return to that wordless space where past and future interface.

This life is just a shabby porch to a magnificent mansion. I'm so happy that I'm goin' to heaven!

HARVEST IS RIPE: START TALKIN'

Broken people make the best messengers of grace (because they need it)— that's how they ace.

The harvest is ripe to preach--It's obvious so don't pull back but speak out against, beseech.

Some gifts are passed down through the genes. It's amazing but my dad did what I do from his teens.

Everyone has different predispositions and proclivities--the good and the bad:

THE TRUTH ABOUT PEOPLE

genes from mom and dad.

The talented are no more talented due to sin. That's the way it always is for a lush, loser, has-been.

We all have talents, we all have quirks. Once we overcome the latter, out comes our marvelous works.

It's a spout: either it comes out or it doesn't. Never force it-- impatience brings ruin all of a sudden.

Traumatic brain chemicals block nutrients to the cells. So not only are we crazier we age faster--oh well.

Terrible trauma floods brain chemicals we get addicted to. You must say to those memories: pooh!

CNN and NBC are both belly up! Those tyrannical, sycophantic collaborators bore falsehood non-stop.

They got off on being mean: Arrogant too, these nasty government thugs and fiends in their teams.

It'll all turn out in your favor--wait and see! Everything you went through until now was part of His scheme.

TURN IT ALL OFF: NOW HAVE HIGHER THOUGHTS

Why you watchin' that stupid show when it's all inside, ya know? To write, just look out the window.

God took me outa the whole mess and placed me on a rock. Repentance was the key to such Luck.

It's the creative act put in you before your birth that should fill you with joy-- explore like a toy.

Marriage is sayin: "all the rest can go to hell. I'm with the One and all else is irrelevant and small".

Any man who talks nicer to other women than to his wife is an abuser. Women

THE TRUTH ABOUT PEOPLE

are psychic you loser.

Music instantly hooks me to higher planes. From the cradle on I learned how it happily dulled my pains.

Poetry is highest cuz--when it comes to words—less is more. It's about impact (not being a bore).

Be a throwback to an earlier time in your genetic history--a true lady/gentleman is a mystery.

CUT OFF OUTER FOR MAGNETISM

Cutting off the outer also increases your personal magnetism: attraction, no more boring inaction.

Resistance builds muscle, so the resistances you've faced made you the greatest since sins were erased.

To find a gold mine, clear the mind. For it's all in you, a rare find. If to this you're blind, stop filling time.

Alcohol is a conduit to the devil who comes in through human weakness then knocks you down a level.

Old grudges steal your life. They ruin forever (but not for the other) while causing heartbreak and strife.

Sh*t-shots are behaviors intended to incur anxiety in the other--remarks, ogling women or whatever.

I like how it uglifies before it heals--their attack precedes your victory over these mean heels.

NOW LISTEN TO NO ONE

Once you've made up your mind, listen to no one. The time has come to shut them all out (keep none).

If you can get past the embarrassment you'll find the pearl inside. This is how it works, bonafide.

THE TRUTH ABOUT PEOPLE

You can't just suffer truth all day long. You gotta create your own reality like a king on his throne.

Enontiodromia: all converts to it's opposite. From demonic sinner to happy saint is the composite.

It's called perseverence: God be with you until the very end--each day and moment your best friend.

Just as one goes out another comes in. Closing doors leaves a space whether for jobs or a new friend.

It's what I do: try to make sense of things all day. I was born to do this and it's so much fun, hurray.

Compulsive rhyming is the need for order as the words fit together by meaning but also sound, yet shorter.

How to know the foe: You gotta draw him out--be nice, mean or whatever to show he's the worst ever.

Systems Theory: We get ugly and draw their ire, then heal (beautify) and they're seen as the liar.

God doesn't say "You can do it!" but rather "it is finished". Imagine that--He's done it all, sis.

What I do isn't tangible, it just makes you think. That is the basis of therapy: you finally see the finks.

This goes way past them so say what you want anyway. You're making a new dent in your own way.

IGNORE MERE APPEARANCES AND CIRCUMSTANCES

Though it's all going to hell around us we can still succeed. It's A Tale of Two Cities if from sin we're freed.

Though dead, it was them who shaped you. Though gone forever, their influence is the cue making you blue.

THE TRUTH ABOUT PEOPLE

They hated her for her sins so instead of repenting (ending their hatred) she caved in, glory faded.

It was all the devil so why go back to any part of it? Joy spirit: go on to a bright future and don't fear it.

Wear a jacket then no matter what you did you always look nice and they'll remember your advice.

I'm not the only one hating having my picture taken. It's a soul snatcher as the spirit's forsaken.

Put it all in the same bag: insanity. It can happen to anyone temporarily so now just be happy.

WHEN POETS DIE

When poets die you still have their words. It's all about copy when describing all the human herds.

If you don't like it just leave. I'm giving you my view and it's all for free so just drop me, please.

They're cruel not knowing what they're doing and Satan uses the weak and it's you he'll be abusing.

You have great zeal and I like your style so keep it up--we should all be spreading info to rank and file.

By forgiving your thief you'll be given tenfold the stolen amount. Action-reaction: God fills your account.

Insanity is: a neuropathway in the brain creating behavior reinforced with each thought of the pain.

Pets are neurotic from mal-adapting to owners. They're always healthy when loved (they're not loners).

Our pets are our friends. Adopt them: accept them as family and please take them to the end.

THE TRUTH ABOUT PEOPLE

Happy homelife is the greatest serenity as divine order creates synchronicity in cosmic serendipity.

It's hard to reconcile predestination with free will. Either way God will take you through to the end still.

Because genius is a rarity, don't crave popularity. Pearls before swine: they trample all verity.

RELEASE OBSTRUCTION, SUCCESS

A born leader will be hated. God knew this, it was fated. Though belated it'll all roll out: what He created.

Thank you God for this work You've given me to do. It's so amazing and fascinating to me too!

I was dying, approaching the end of the tunnel. I impeached Jesus and He brought me back as a funnel.

A merciful God meets our failures with His grace, our guilts with His forgiveness. Through Him we are sinless.

A man's worst enemies are in his own household. They could change but most get more obdurate when old.

You dug a ditch for me to fall into but haha you fell into it yourself now don't be blue you cad/shrew.

Now let's talk about your kin. Are they your friends? Doubtful, bible says your worst enemies reside therein.

Liberals aren't family. Liberals are loyal to nobody unless there's money.

What a waste if you die from stress because you couldn't forgive. Let God take care of it so you can give.

Saddest thing about betrayal is it never comes from enemies but friends and loved ones despite our pleas.

THE TRUTH ABOUT PEOPLE

It was actually the devil who brought me to God cuz I was so disgusted I sought the highest and was awed.

I struggled with it for years, they drove me to tears: Let God put you up front and them in the rears.

God chooses the foolish things of the world to confound the wise, so be foolish but sin you must <u>despise</u>.

HOLOCAUST DENIAL IS HATE SPEECH

The Holocaust was the mass murder of millions under the Nazi regime and the youth don't know about it.

Holocaust-denial is HATE SPEECH. Tho' it's often illegal in Europe it's actually growing here in the states.

As we saw in WWII a targeted ethnic group should never rely on another nation to save them.

Nazi Germany had 150 different uniforms. So you see it wasn't just brutality it relates to narcissism.

When they get free stuff they don't build character and things only get worse/they don't appreciate it.

The mamby-pamby soft snowflake youth complain about nil not knowing or caring millions were killed.

If youth don't care about millions of abortions why care about millions killed in a prior generation?

Holocaust-deniers are liars and collaborators. It's shocking/should be stamped out soon as you hear it.

Holocaust students stand up to negative stereotyping and challenge incorrect or biased information.

Holocaust was so horrible/ghastly/beyond the pale they're afraid to teach it when kids have already failed.

THE TRUTH ABOUT PEOPLE

FREE SPEECH IS INCITEMENT

Left doesn't advance the news often but sees events as opportunities to advance socialism.

Europe's ahead of America in nationalism building. We're going thru global fascism see.

Free speech is now bad--it could be incitement. All their power is going to shutting down our rights.

They shut down all the speech they don't like as "misinformation" and what arrogance son.

They didn't outright ban me but just suppressed my reach. I don't know which is more deadly.

LEFT: revolutionary aggression, top-down censorship, seeing any dissident as an immoral person.

Soon individual rights take a backseat to equity: what the collective requires strips us immediately.

BEAUTY IS SELF-DISCIPLINE

Beauty from self-discipline is a good thing. Must know you deserve it whether you dance, write or sing.

Thank God for your bloated belly cuz it's time to fast. Thank God for weight gain, now have a blast.

It's not enough to eat fruit and rice you gotta fast too. It's the Trump Card which always works for you.

If something's caught in the line you gotta fast to streamline. Don't eat, resist, no cheat.

Narrow things down. The cold and Christmas seasons are the same: orange, red, maroon, burgundy, grape.

THE TRUTH ABOUT PEOPLE

Leave cold colors for the spring and summer: blue, green, aqua, lime, purple, colors of space out there.

All that meat is PP: pugnacity-procreative. That's why he's always wanting sex like a savage.

Don't be a glutton. **EAT, THEN DON'T EAT.** It's as simple as that. Elegant people don't snack.

BULIMIA KILLS

Karen Carpenter shoulda just stayed home and made records not tour all over: ANOREXIA.

Touring all over the world, having to adapt to people after being sheltered: symptoms roll out.

Bulimia kills. There are very few elderly anorexics, most die by their forties, it's the. devil.

I love the magic of glucagon but auto-immunity is triggered as foods go acid: REFLUX.

Had grape juice way too soon after a high protein/fat meal then acid reflux was all I could feel.

Much less quantity is needed with fauna--animal fat--so that's adjusted to avoid pain/trauma.

Fruit juice/cliff bar in morning then later a little fauna or just a piece of cheese is enough for ya'.

Or do you wanna go back to cutting all those salads and digesting all that fiber? Bummer.

The ladies of the fifties were wafer thin and this is how they did it: a boiled egg, a piece cheese.

FAUNA-FASTING

THE TRUTH ABOUT PEOPLE

Cheese omelet is good one day but inflames the next. Must ROTATE so immune won't react.

You're gonna get real skinny on the Old Lady Diet. You won't be in pain but now high as a kite!

A couple grapes, a piece cheese--that's how it's gotten with me. Not a big meal see.

The Old Lady Diet solution is simple: eat less, release the exhilaration of REAL ENERGY.

A little carb, a little fat, a little protein--what else do you need? No need to trash/bulk eat.

We can't get skinny like the 70's due to global changes but we can fast/get close to the angels.

Paleoscience shows man is like a cat--he needs FAT. Not a lot, that's what makes it so fab.

Not an 8 egg omelet with a lb. of cheese in it--we learn by our pain mistakes on things like that.

Fruits & vegetables seems most obvious but genius doesn't trust the obvious, just facts.

I ate truckloads of fruits & grains to become a shriveled mess but fat brought me back to my best.

DIGESTIVE ISSUES

To boomers: As years go on you can't digest like you used to thus the over-the-counters too.

I'm sick of spending the whole night in agony cuz I screwed up again after crossing lines.

I wanna LOOK and FEEL good every moment and that doesn't come from the taste trip friend.

THE TRUTH ABOUT PEOPLE

Sbowflakes hate all rules. You're banned from diet groups if believing in discipline, by fools.

MAGIC GLUCAGONS

Scrambled eggs, go fight a war. Or would you fight it or run a race after having cauliflower?

The skinny went right for the meat, cheese and eggs and never had vegetables in their frig.

By eating fat/no carbs **GLUCAGONS** is elevated [opposite to insulin] to delete water retention.

When **GLUCAGONS** is elevated we streamline, fat-burn, water-excrete and hunger-delete.

Glucagons eliminates inflammation--even acid reflux, no more pain--and made me sane again.

Elevated glucagons is A.K.A. "fat-adapted" when energy comes from burning not sugar but fat.

FRUIT AND FAT
First meal: nutbutter [spoon theory] just cuz it's easy for a workaholic or recovered anorexic.

Meal Two at my desk: frozen grapes. Nothing more delicious and refreshing, to noon.

Meal three: relax with family. Fish, shrimp, piece cheese, salad, vegetable in sauce.

Vegetable like cauliflower with cheese sauce is a good choice or lunch, it satiates but no ouch.

Nutbutter lasts two hours and for a workaholic it's the ultimate fast food good for you too.

Starchy breakfasts put me to sleep then I choke. Nutbutters and fruit elevate you up.

THE TRUTH ABOUT PEOPLE

Cliff Bars for elite athletes. Never caused a problem and gets the job done for morning errands.

QUEEN OF THE FRUITS

Grapes are the QUEEN of the fruits. All energy comes from grape carbon and I like frozen too.

Protein/fat for lunch: I like fish, shrimp, a little cheese, a weekly omelet, melted cheese with salsa.

It took a life to see a need for daily protein in a beauty scheme: just fruit was a bad scene.

Eating fruit all day, no way. I don't wanna eat anyway, protein/fat allows long fasts between ok.

Americans are so out of touch. I look at his face and all I see is "Joe's Garage" not a nice hat.

DIGESTIVE ISSUES

Even avocado has fiber in it, I had a gut ache for two days from it. Irony: shrimp fixes it.

Green veggie cellulose gives me gut aches. Who needs this? Cheese/shrimp works best.

The need-for-fiber myth made ant-acids/laxatives billion dollar industries like they planned it see.

I do so much better on a piece of cheese than a cauliflower, I want that saturated fat sir.

Bananas and avocados: latex allergy. Greens: add to that goitrogens, oxylates, nightshades see.

A vegetable meal leaves me in pain or a feeling of boring mental nothingness in the main.

THE TRUTH ABOUT PEOPLE

Nightshade allergies: tomatoes hurt, potatoes hurt and forget eggplant or paprika of course.

I'm not gonna tell you to eat your kale and all that crap. It gives you goitrogens and is dangerous.

And what of the anti-nutrients in grains? They aren't harmless by any means even the beans.

Grape juice and shrimp. Breaking all the rules but it feels just right & no need for green s**t.

DATE AND FRUIT SMOOTHIES

I've given up getting calories by stuffing with starches. I get them naturally with fat added.

New breakfast favorite: blend frozen mango and dates. Wow! Incredibly delicious/glycogen for the day.

Put dates in a mango smoothie to froth it up, not nut-butters which increase glycation with fat.

Living where everyone burns I can attest to this: have an air filter in every room for when toxins hit.

Put the music on and all cells open up. I explode in wonderment, it's always the way I daily start.

You create the kind of enriched environment [EE] where the cats and dogs wanna hang out.

My new eye shadow palette came today and I'm thrilled with it. I love make up/romance ambience.

Feminists attack normal females for shaving legs or make-up but when it's a tranny they're not averse to it.

Synthetic Creep: If "smartwool" is 10% nylon the chemically sensitive like myself are done.

THE TRUTH ABOUT PEOPLE

It's near impossible to find 100% wool or cotton. It's all cut with synthetics triggering autoimmune.

Quit fishin' for something on net that's relevant or will give you a buzz. Get offa that thing, home is all.

As a trumpeter salsero I met many people and we had a ball. I never was so high in my life: STOKED!

They noted the superiority of my style/substance so they sought to emulate but failed being third rate.

PORK IN THE POWERLESS

The powerless woman subconsciously thinks the only way to absorb the world's impact is to be fat.

To lose all that fat would leave her defenseless though in any fight she wouldn't have a chance.

The physical allergy to alcohol manifested as PANIC in the middle of the night or whenever not lit.

Never thought I'd win the Taste Trip where I wanted to eat everything in the universe, but I did.

It was emotional hunger, not physical. Trying to fill the empty void inside or to cover it over, full.

I can only eat ONCE in a day or there's hell to pay. It's gotta be early or I choke in my sleep ok.

The denser the food the longer the transit time/energy used to digest. Juicy fruit is the easiest.

The very idea of eating a steak for dinner then sleeping is like killing me after the choking at midnight.

How many tens of thousands die of choking in their sleep but it's listed as "died peacefully in sleep".

THE TRUTH ABOUT PEOPLE

As the sphincter muscle relaxes with age it allows food back up to the throat and you choke ok.

KEEP A LEDGER/NEVER FORGET

Keep a ledger so you never forget: all that trouble came from sin, all the good stuff from repentance.

Don't say you're a writer, BE a writer. Don't say you're a singer, BE a singer. No image-magic faker.

Continue to live a good life and you'll never return to that dungeon again--the consequences of sin.

"What you did" folds into collective consciousness then it is lost in the whole world/historical mess.

Don't worry cuz if you walk the straight/narrow not the carnal/crooked life's no longer wretched.

Trump's the only one who can save us from this mess that increases by the minute of the blessed.

THE IMPORTANCE OF LEISURE

You're OFF. You MUST take the day off for only would-be genius has an incapacity for leisure.

Genius is marked by his capacity for LEISURE, a treasure to get his batteries back up I swear.

What are you gonna do, throw yourself on the funeral pyre of your husband? A woman for survival goes forward and plans.

A woman for survival goes forward/plans. Men die early, being alone sux, you're a great add.

How could Hope go back to fat cheater Liam when she has adorable thin cut Thomas available?

THE TRUTH ABOUT PEOPLE

I kept waiting for another destructive jam to happen but it never did cuz I had finally, truly repented.

Repent and life goes smoothly finally. Stay put [not ready to let it go] and you're punished daily.

There's no need for endless apprehensions making you grey in the night, everything's all right.

We'll just have to rely on the fact thoughts are things and you're picking up on all I'm thinking.

If God is with us no matter how impossible it seems He will give us the victory.

I've been physically attacked for my ideas so of course I don't go anywhere or see anybody.

NEVER give a kitten/puppy to someone to get their approval. That's the wrong reason Mabel.

ASK OF ME THE LORD SAYS

Ask of Me and I'll give the nations as your inheritance, the earth for your possession. Psa 2: 8

I may be a sinner like him and her but my works are perfect so just look at that please sir.

Now I know it's too late. You lost your soul, you'll never change--you chose that life instead of love.

Gotta write the book first THEN you make the money. You gamble your whole life on it honey.

It's 60,000 self-standing proverbs in 130 books in all languages for the whole world to know it.

The new Social Psychology has a formula with 60,000 proverbs of the new paradigm/artistic gem.

They've been called Self Standing Proverbs, available in all languages for the world's benefit.